The Trinity Untangled

Making Sense of a Sensible Doctrine

The Trinity Untangled

Making Sense of a Sensible Doctrine

by

Kenneth N. Myers

Mayeux Press
DENISON, TEXAS

The Trinity Untangled

Myers, Kenneth Neal, 1959-
The Trinity Untangled/Kenneth N. Myers

1. Christian Theology

Cover design: Michael Peterson

Published by Mayeux Press
561 Bailey Drive, Denison TX 75021

For Lamia

Acknowledgements

This book would not be possible without the the encouragement and support of Daniel & Julie Walter, Mark & Lori Frimann, my parents, and the partners of Graceworks Teaching Ministry.

Thank you to my wife Shirley for being the best wife in the history of the world.

Thank you to Mac Culver, Daniel Walter, Chris Linebarger, Rusty Matheny and Nathan Haydon for their valuable comments as the book was being written.

Thank you to Kenneth Tanner for being on the same page.

Table of Contents

Preface

Why Write Another Book On The Trinity?

I have written a number of books on subjects which are dear to my heart (why on earth write a book on something you don't care about?), but the subject of the Holy Trinity is perhaps the one closest to my heart and longest a part of my reflection and study. I have devoutly studied this topic for thirty six years, have sporadically written about it, taught seminars on it, preached on it, and discussed it privately for hours on end. There are two reasons I believe this book is important.

Basic Christian Ignorance

Along with the doctrines of the deity and humanity of Jesus Christ, the doctrine of the Holy Trinity is foundational to the Christian faith (and these foundational doctrines are intrinsically related). Christians can and do hold many disparate beliefs about important things and still remain within the pale of biblical and faithful Christianity. How did this world begin? How will this world end? What are the mechanics of how we are saved? What, precisely, is the Church? What about the sacraments? What is the correct structure of leadership within the Church? How should we worship God? All these are important questions, and thoughtful Christians usually have a well reasoned conviction for the answers they give, but they can differ from one another and still remain faithful Christians.

But when we come to the most crucial and foundational beliefs of the Christian faith, too many believers are willing to simply say, "It's beyond me. I just believe it," while devoting all of forty-five minutes of their lives to contemplating or studying or attempting to understand the most basic doctrine of all - the doctrine of God himself.

I once had an old and seasoned Episcopal priest quote Psalm 131.1 to me, "O LORD, my heart is not lifted up; my eyes are not raised too high; I do not occupy myself with things too great and too marvelous for me," and then proceed to tell me that I had no business delving in to the complexities of understanding the Trinity. This from a man who took it as his responsibility to guard and teach the faith of the Church!

Charles Spurgeon, the famous Baptist preacher of the 19th century, wrote, "In attempting to define the Trinity, or unveil the essence of Divinity, many men have lost themselves: here great ships have foundered. What have we to do in such a sea with our frail skiffs?"[1]

To which any heretical cultist might respond, "Aha! See! That Trinity business of yours makes no sense at all. You are afraid to even reason it out. You can't fight your way out of a wet paper bag when it comes to your doctrine of God because you are wrong!" And then they would proceed to tell us that Jesus is *not* God himself come in the flesh, or that God the Father and God the Son are two different beings, or that the Father, Son and Holy Spirit are "God" only in the sense that as three different beings they all belong to some kind of very exclusive God Club.

Because pastors and teachers and bishops and priests have not equipped the people of God with a solid understanding of God himself, many Christians easily fall prey to the cultists knocking on their doors. But even if the knock never comes, far too many Christians embrace various

[1] Spurgeon, Charles, Treasury of David, Volume 1, Houston, Pilgrim Publishers, 1983, p. 13.

wrong or even heretical notions all on their own, as though the ideas, which were never actually preached or taught in their churches, were derived by a kind of spiritual and intellectual osmosis. The two most common errors that are all too often found in Christian circles also happen to be two of the oldest errors: tritheism and modalism.

Tritheism: I have spent my life around Christians who call themselves Trinitarian, insist they don't believe in three different Gods, and then proceed to explain the Trinity precisely as three different Gods. The Father does one thing, the Son behaves differently, and the Holy Spirit is just a nebulous entity we don't quite get. In their minds, in eternity when we stand before God we will see an old man with a white beard, a young man (let's say, about thirty three years old) with a brown beard, and a bird or a glow or whatever that nebulous Holy Spirit "looks like." This even effects their understanding of salvation itself, and in far too many cases Christians mistakenly understand salvation as God the Son saving us *from* God the Father and his fury. There is an intellectual disconnect between their thesis ("I believe in one God") and their explanation ("There are really three different Gods") and yet all of this is jumbled together and presented as the Christian doctrine of the Trinity. Well, it isn't.

Modalism: To avoid this extreme of tritheism masquerading as the Christian doctrine of the Trinity, other believers hang on to the pendulum for dear life as it swings to the far opposite side. They say, "Of course there are not three Gods! Why, that would be the despicable heresy of tritheism! There is only one God, and he manifests himself in three different ways." They go on to describe God as a kind of actor on the stage who wears three different masks, depending on which scene he is in. In scene one, he wears the Father mask. Scene one is usually the Old Testament. In scene two, he puts on the Son mask. Scene two is usually the four Gospels. Then in scene three, he wears the Holy Spirit mask. Scene three is usually the Church Age, beginning with the book of Acts. One God, three different manifestations or roles. This also is not the Christian doctrine of the Trinity.

The first reason I am writing this book is to give the reader a solid, biblical, historic, and comprehendible understanding of the Christian doctrine of the Holy Trinity.

Between A Rock And A Soft Place

I don't mean to suggest that there aren't any good books out there which do precisely that. There are (and I will refer to some of them throughout this book, and list them at the end). There are some brilliant theologians from the past who have written extensively on the Trinity. There are some magnificent thinkers from the last hundred years who have done the same. And they are all pointing to the same truth and the same understanding. These writers and their works are rocks; they are giant boulders. And most people won't read them. The reality is these writings are just too deep, too complex and too enormous for the average Christian (or even the average clergyman) to read. Good stuff; no, *great* stuff; but inaccessible to the majority of thoughtful Christians.

On the other hand, there is what I would call the "soft place." Christians in their search for understanding the Trinity aren't stuck between a rock and a hard place. On the opposite side of the rock is a very soft place. Too many books written on the Trinity today are either so simplistic (soft) as to say nothing at all, or even worse, very wrong in the ideas they present.

My goal in writing this book is to provide something that is beyond milk for spiritual babes; something that is meaty, and yet chewable (I mean, I'm all for good beef jerky that you have to gnaw on, but sometimes a nice medium-rare tenderloin that you can cut with a fork is just what the body needs). I aim to provide a study of the Holy Trinity that is deep enough to swim in, and yet isn't so far out into the deep blue sea that the waves would overwhelm the inexperienced swimmer. I hope to present a tome that can be understood by anyone who gives it a thoughtful read and which will, at the same time, contain biblical and historic theological reflections that will give the reader pause, cause them to contemplate, see new things (actually old things), and perhaps dig deeper on their own.

G.K. Chesterton wrote a magnificent article in 1904 titled, *Why I Believe In Christianity*. Always a writer who draws our attention to paradox, he contrasted the religions of Islam and Christianity:

> Christianity, which is a very mystical religion, has nevertheless been the religion of the most practical section of mankind. It has far more paradoxes than the Eastern philosophies, but it also builds far better roads.

The Moslem has a pure and logical conception of God, the one Monistic Allah. But he remains a barbarian in Europe, and the grass will not grow where he sets his foot. The Christian has a Triune God, "a tangled trinity," which seems a mere capricious contradiction in terms. But in action he bestrides the earth, and even the cleverest Eastern can only fight him by imitating him first. The East has logic and lives on rice. Christendom has mysteries - and motor cars.[2]

He is right, of course. We have mysteries - and motor cars (if he could only see us now!). We also have "a tangled Trinity." It is my sincere hope that this book will help with that.

---

[2] Chesterton, Gilbert Keith, *The Collected Works of G.K. Chesterton, Vol. 1*, San Francisco, Ignatius Press, 1986, p. 382.

Introduction

What you hold in your hands is a mystery book.

In the Bible, mystery (*mysterion*) doesn't mean a puzzle to be solved, like an Agatha Christie murder mystery, but a secret which is revealed.

The thing is, when Jesus uses this word (which he does only once, the singular time referenced by all three synoptic Gospels, Mt. 13.11, Mk. 4.11, Lu. 8.10: "To you it has been given to know the *secrets* of the kingdom of heaven, but to them it has not been given."), or when Paul uses this word (which he does frequently - for example, 1 Co. 15.51: "Behold! I tell you a *mystery*. We shall not all sleep, but we shall all be changed."), the secret which is revealed is a heavenly secret: something previously unknown, and really unknowable by our own initiative, now made known by God himself. The ideas of mystery and revelation are closely woven together. These mysteries that the New Testament mention are things that cannot be discovered by human reason or emotion, they are things that God himself reveals to us by his grace and his own desire for union with humanity.

The word, *mysterion*, ends up getting used in Christian writings to also apply to the sacraments - the mysteries that come from heaven and bring a heavenly reality to us here on earth.

Perhaps the best definition of the word *mysterion* that I have come across is, "something that cannot be put into words." You get a glimpse of it, you attempt to lay hold of it, you experience it, you love it, but you can't *describe* it - not really, not fully. You just have to embrace it. Embrace the mystery.

A mystery is something we cannot put into words. Something we cannot describe. But that doesn't stop us from trying. And all theology is at the bottom line an attempt to put into words that which cannot be described. Nowhere is this more true than when we are talking about God himself. He is simply beyond our words. He is beyond our comprehension. He is beyond our ability to encounter and experience by our own strength. He is transcendent (more about this later). And yet, because we love God, because we are drawn to him, because we want to know him more and know more about him, we simply cannot resist talking about him.

Who are you? *Who in the world **are** you?* Good Lord, who *are* you? These are the questions Moses asked God when he encountered the burning bush, and these are the questions we all ask in our hearts.

We want to know who someone *is* that we love. We want to know everything we can know about them. To ultimately understand God is an impossibility, because he is transcendent and above and beyond us, but we want to know him because we love him.

So, let us speak about the unspeakable. Let us describe the indescribable. Let us circumscribe him who is without boundaries. We shall, of course, fail, but we cannot help but do it.

Chapter One

The Punchline

I hate jigsaw puzzles. My wife loves them but they drive me nuts. She goes out and gets a 500 piece puzzle and over the course of weeks spends hours putting the thing together. She even has a puzzle app on her iPad. That stuff drives me crazy. Far from relaxing me, it takes me to the frustrated brink of a heart attack.

Stories that are puzzling, on the other hand, delight me. Guy de Maupassant and O. Henry are favorites of mine. Give me a book with plot twists and surprise endings, or a movie with several confusing threads that tie together toward the end, and I'm a happy camper.

When I teach seminars on the subject of the Holy Trinity I am guilty of saving the "Aha!" moment until the middle of the seminar or maybe toward the end. I love laying out several seemingly disparate lines of thought for the people, then tying them all together and watching the light bulb turn on in their minds. Like Hannibal Smith used to say, "I love it when a plan comes together." But this book is going to be different. Instead of laying out chapter after chapter of supporting material then drawing the conclusion toward the end, I'm going to give away the punchline in the first chapter.

So, you don't even have to read this whole book to "get" what I'm saying, if you don't want to. I mean, I hope you *will* read it all, and I promise there will still be some light bulbs that turn on. In fact the bulb that gets turned on in this first chapter will get much brighter in later chapters, but you can get the main point of the book by just finishing this chapter.

So let's cut to the chase. Here is the punchline: there is only one God, and he is manifest to us as God the Son.

I am only going to give the very briefest of headlines in these next few paragraphs, and unpack the ideas throughout the rest of the book.

First, there is only one God. The foundational statement of the Judeo-Christian tradition is Deuteronomy 6.4: "Hear, O Israel: The Lord our God, the Lord is one." When Jesus was asked what was the greatest commandment, he quoted this verse. Simply put, Christians don't believe in thousands, or hundreds, or even three gods. We believe in one God. Period. End of discussion. Whatever else we may say about the godhead, the Trinity, or the divine nature, the core truth is that there is only one true God. Any time anyone has ever encountered God - whether it be Adam in Genesis, or Moses in Exodus, or some Native American in the middle of 14th century North America, or some African tribesman 4,000 years ago - *anytime anyone anywhere* has encountered God, it is the one true God who has been encountered. There simply are no others.

Second, this one true God reveals himself strictly and only in what we call God the Son. This God the Son became flesh in the person of Jesus of Nazareth, but from eternity past until eternity future (if those phrases even make sense, which they don't), the only way we see or know or encounter God the Father is through the Son. John describes this truth in the Prologue to his Gospel, John 1. Note carefully the three things he is saying:

"In the beginning was the Word, and the Word was with God, and the Word was God…And the Word became flesh and dwelt among us… No one has ever seen God; the only God, who is at the Father's side, he has made him known" (John 1.1, 14, 18).

Here, then, are the three things John tells us:

- The Word *is* God. Think of it like this: the Word is the "projected" or "published" or "manifest" or "brought forth" aspect of God. The Word is the *revelation* of the invisible God. And so while there is some kind of mysterious *distinction* between the Father and the Word ("the Word was *with* God"), at the same time there is a complete *unity* ("the Word *was* God). We will explore this in more detail, but suffice it to say now that the Word *is* God.

- This Word became flesh in the person of Jesus within our time and history. The other Gospels tell the Christmas story in more earthly terms, but in the womb of the Virgin Mary the Word took on flesh. He was born, lived, died, and rose again. Jesus *is* the Word become flesh. God become flesh.

- No one has ever seen God the Father, but through this Word the Father is revealed to us. If the Word simply *is* the revelation of the Father, we can say in an almost silly, simplistic way, "No one has ever seen the invisible God except by God's revelation."

Let me say it like this. Any time anyone has ever encountered God - whether it be Adam in Genesis, or Moses in Exodus, or some Native American in the middle of 14th century North America, or some African tribesman 4,000 years ago - *anytime anyone anywhere* has encountered God, it is the revealing Word making the invisible Father known. There simply is no other revelation of the one, true, invisible God. The Word *is* the revelation of the Father. And in Jesus of Nazareth, God himself joined himself to our humanity and to the stuff of his own creation. Forever.

Now, let's unpack the bags, shall we?

Chapter Two

Defining God

Defining God is a silly business right from the start, because it is simply impossible to define the One who is beyond all definition. But the Christian faith is that this One has chosen of his own volition to make himself known. The transcendent One has become immanent, he has revealed himself and come close to us, and through this revelation we can say some things about God, about who he is and what he is like. In standard systematic theology, these descriptions are called "the attributes of God," and in this chapter we will briefly look at eight attributes or characteristics.

Singular

The place to start in understanding the nature of God is the simplicity or singularity of God himself. God is one. Deuteronomy 6.4 is the first verse Jewish children memorized. If Christian kids are taught John 3.16 as the verse that capsulizes the whole New Testament, Jewish boys and girls were taught Deuteronomy 6.4 as the verse that capsulized everything Judaism was about. The verse, called the *Shema*, simply says, "Hear O Israel, the Lord our God: The Lord is one."

One day Jesus was talking to a group of men about things theological, and a scribe saw that he was answering well, so though he would weigh in with his own question, perhaps to trip up Jesus in an argument:

One of the scribes...asked him, "Which commandment is the most important of all?" Jesus answered, "The most important is, 'Hear, O Israel: The Lord our God, the Lord is one. And you shall love the Lord your God with all your heart and with all your soul and with all your mind and with all your strength.' The second is this: 'You shall love your neighbor as yourself.' There is no other commandment greater than these" (Mark 12.28-32).

Whatever else Christianity teaches about God, the foundational truth is this: God is one. There are not millions of gods as some Eastern religions hold, there is not a *pleroma* of gods or a hierarchy of gods as some of the Gnostics held, there are not gods mating and making babies who grow up to be gods as the Greeks and Romans held, and there are not three Gods as some of the heretical "Christian" groups held. There is one God. Period. End of story.

Holy

One of the words most frequently associated with God in the Old Testament is *holy:*

> 1 Samuel 2:2 There is none *holy* like the LORD: for there is none besides you; there is no rock like our God.

> Isaiah 6.1-3: In the year that King Uzziah died I saw the Lord sitting upon a throne, high and lifted up; and the train of his robe filled the temple. Above him stood the seraphim. Each had six wings: with two he covered his face, and with two he covered his feet, and with two he flew. And one called to another and said: *"Holy, holy, holy* is the Lord of hosts; the whole earth is full of his glory!"

> Psalm 71.22: I will also praise you with the harp for your faithfulness, O my God; I will sing praises to you with the lyre, O *Holy One of Israel.*

When we hear the word holy, we tend to translate it in our minds as *moral* - "Good old Joe doesn't go out partying or run with the wrong bunch. He's a really holy guy." But that isn't what it means, really. The Hebrew word for holy is *qadosh* (the Greek is *hagios*), and it doesn't speak to morality, but to *separateness*. It speaks of "the innermost description of God's nature,"[3] and perhaps the best English word to use to translate *qadosh* is *unique*.

To say that God is holy is to say that he is separate from everything else that exists. He is infinite, all else is finite. He is uncreated, all else is created. He is completely other. He is transcendent. You see, of course, how this connects to the idea of him being singular. To be unique requires oneness.

---

[3] "As already in the OT, e.g., in the prophets, the ἅγιος predicate is referred to the person of God. Indeed, it contains the innermost description of God's nature (Is. 6:3). Thus the Trisagion recurs in the song of praise of the four beasts in Rev. 4:8." (Kittel, TDNT, v. 1, p. 100).

Theologically used, anything else called holy is so called because of its relationship to God, whether that be holy ground, a holy people, a holy vessel, or a holy place. A thing becomes holy because it is *separated* out for God, and is somehow related to the unique, transcendent, singular God himself. But if we are speaking ontologically (that is, regarding the nature of a thing itself), only God is truly holy.

Uncreated Creator

The story of our faith begins with creation: "In the beginning, God created the heavens and the earth" (Genesis 1.1). This completely unique, completely other, self-existing One made everything else that exists. To put it simply, there are only two categories in the whole world: the divine (God himself), and everything else.

Isaiah draws the distinction between God and everything else when he writes, "Have you not known? Have you not heard? The Lord is the everlasting God, *the Creator of the ends of the earth*. He does not faint or grow weary; his understanding is unsearchable" (Isaiah 40.28), and Saint Paul echoes him when he preached the Gospel at the Areopagus in Athens: "*The God who made the world and everything in it*, being Lord of heaven and earth, does not live in temples made by man, nor is he served by human hands, as though he needed anything, since he himself gives to all mankind life and breath and everything" (Acts. 17.24, 25).

Unchanging (Immutable)

The other ancient religions of the world (be they Greek, Roman, Eastern or some local tribal religion) saw the gods as fickle, even downright moody. Any particular god could wake up on the wrong side of the bed and be downright mean when only the day before he had blessed the people with rain or victory in battle or whatever. These gods were constantly having to be appeased, placated, and sacrificed to just to win their favor (and unfortunately, some of this pagan thinking has crept back into some Christian circles, but it isn't the Gospel).

If God is "that than which nothing greater can be conceived" as Anselm said, then he is unchanging. He can't get *better*. The prophet Malachi wrote, "For I the Lord *do not change*; therefore you, O children of Jacob, are not consumed" (Malachi 3.6).

The New Testament confirms the unchangeability of God. The writer of Hebrews tells us, "So when God desired to show more convincingly to the heirs of the promise *the unchangeable character* of his purpose, he guaranteed it with an oath, so that by two unchangeable things, in which it is impossible for God to lie, we who have fled for refuge might have strong encouragement to hold fast to the hope set before us" (Hebrews 6.17,18). But perhaps James, the brother of Jesus, best describes God's immutability: "Every good gift and every perfect gift is from above, coming down from the Father of lights *with whom there is no variation or shadow due to change*" (James 1.17). God is, we are told, "the same, yesterday, today, and forever" (Hebrews 13.8).

Christians, then, have a great treasure of comfort in this truth. God is dependable. He is faithful. He is consistent. He doesn't change. You don't have to wonder if he is going to be different today than he was yesterday.[4]

All Knowing (Omniscient)

Because God is unchanging, he doesn't *grow* by adding new knowledge. He knows all, already. From the beginning to the end, from *before* the beginning and forever, God knows all. We humans are in a constant flux of change. As creatures of time, we add new knowledge and new experiences (and some of us *forget* as much

---

[4] For more on the unchanging nature of God, see the *Immutability of God, Summa Theologica*, Thomas Aquinas: http://www.newadvent.org/summa/1009.htm.

as we add). But with God, everything is *present,* so to speak. He knows all, he experiences all, in the now. There is no past or present, no change, no flux, no growing or diminishing in his being or his knowing. John wrote, "for whenever our heart condemns us, God is greater than our heart, and *he knows everything*" (1 John 3.20).

All Present (Omnipresent)

When King Solomon dedicated the Temple in Jerusalem, he said, "But will God indeed dwell on the earth? Behold, heaven and the highest heaven cannot contain you; how much less this house that I have built" (1 Kings 8.27). Jeremiah wrote, "Can a man hide himself in secret places so that I cannot see him? Do I not fill heaven and earth?" (Jeremiah 23.24).

How do we, who are locked into space and time, even think about One who isn't? It really is impossible to wrap our minds around it. When we say God is omnipresent, that he is everywhere, the way we tend to think of it is that God is so *big* that he fills all of creation. But this is a disservice to the idea. What we really should think (and it is practically impossible to do so) is that God is completely and fully in all places at the same time. In other words, God is completely and totally here with me, and at the same time he is completely and totally there with you. All of him is everywhere! The Psalmist tried to capture the idea when he wrote, "Where shall I go from your Spirit? Or where shall I flee from your presence? If I make my bed in Sheol, you are there! If I take the wings of the morning and dwell in the uttermost parts of the sea, even there your hand shall lead me, and your right hand shall hold me." (Psalm 139.7-10).

All Powerful (Omnipotent)

That God is all powerful is a given. But at first glance we can't find a single text of the Bible that declares him to be omnipotent. This is, however, a case of a thing being so prevalent, "right under our noses," that we fail to see it at first glance. 58 times in the Bible God is called "Almighty." All mighty. All powerful. The first place he is designated as almighty is Genesis 17.1: "When Abram was ninety-nine years old the Lord appeared to Abram and said to him, "I am *God Almighty*; walk before me, and be blameless." This wasn't some local deity from back home in Ur who was speaking to Abram. This was the One who holds all power, the One who is above all else. Jeremiah would later praise this One by saying, "Ah, Lord God! It is you who have made the heavens and the earth by your great power and by your outstretched arm! *Nothing is too hard for you*" (Jeremiah 32.17).

Eternal

As I have already mentioned, we creatures who are locked in to time and space simply cannot wrap our minds around the idea of God being eternal. We tend to think eternal is just an unlimited measurement of time. But eternity is *outside* time. Eternity existed before time began to be measured. Everything else, and I mean *everything* - angels, humans, trees, rocks, planets, galaxies, pizza, kittens - everything else is limited to time. Things change, things wear out, things come and go. There are stars in the sky that we look at with our naked eye that aren't even there anymore. It has just taken that long for their light to reach us. They are long dead and quiet and dark. Your great great grandparents are gone. You will be gone. Your grandchildren will be gone. Your clothes, your house and your nation will be gone. "They will perish, but you will remain; they will all wear out like a garment. You will change them like a robe, and they will pass away" (Psalm 102.26). But God isn't going anywhere. He is outside time, outside change, outside *becoming* or *un-becoming*. He simply *is*. He is the "I Am."

Isaiah records the words from God, "For thus says the One who is high and lifted up, *who inhabits eternity, whose name is*

Holy: 'I dwell in the high and holy place, and also with him who is of a contrite and lowly spirit, to revive the spirit of the lowly, and to revive the heart of the contrite'" (Isaiah 57.15). But it is Paul who breaks into praise for God and pens the most marvelous description of him, wrapping up all these attributes into a single statement: "To the King of the ages, immortal, invisible, the only God, be honor and glory forever and ever. Amen" (1 Timothy 1.17).

This, then, is what the Christian faith teaches us about God. God is singular, completely other, unique, uncreated, unchanging, all knowing, all present, all powerful, and eternal. This is the God we worship. And there aren't three of him.

Where Things Get Messy

There aren't three of him. There aren't three Gods. And this is where things get messy and confusing among Christians, because the witness of Scripture is that these attributes we have described may be attributed to God the Father, and also to God the Son (who came in flesh in the person of Jesus Christ of Nazareth) and to God the Holy Spirit.

How can there be *three* who are truly holy, unique, almighty? How can there be *three* who possess the attributes of the singular I Am, the God who alone inhabits eternity? How can we say that the Father is God, the Son is God, and the Holy Spirit is God and yet insist there is only one God? Ah! Now we are getting to the good stuff!

Chapter Three

Seeing the Invisible God

For the next several paragraphs I'm going to be writing about language. If language bores you, just skip down to the next section. Otherwise, you can humor me, and maybe have some fun thinking about words.

Language in general and words in specific have always fascinated me. We tend to think there is a "right" and "wrong" way of "doing" language, but it all really boils down to culturally imposed rules.

How English speakers speak in the deep South and how they speak in New York may be very different, but neither is right or wrong, they just are.

There is a dialect of English spoken today that linguists call African American Vernacular English, and it is a real dialect of the English language with its own peculiar pronunciations and grammatical rules. In other words, people really *communicate* with one another using it. Non-linguists have another word for it: Ebonics. It originated in the African American subculture of the deep South, and has kinship with other dialects, including the South Louisiana French/ English dialect ("Cajun"). My father's side of the family hails from South Louisiana and I absolutely love how my grandparents used to talk. For example, my grandfather wouldn't say, "The store is down the road two or three miles." Instead he would say, "The store is down the road three or two miles." I heard one Cajun talking about birds and he said, "There must have been five hundred of 'em, I don't know, there may have been *three* hundred!" Of course, he said *tree* instead of *three*.

Ebonics speakers don't say, "I am reading a book." They say, "I be reading a book." Let's talk for a minute about *am* and *be*.

For you English geeks who may be reading this, *am* is a verb, and it is the first person singular present indicative of *be*. Other forms of *be* are *is, are, was, were, been*, and *being*. *Be* means to exist. "To be or not to be, that is the question," Shakespeare famously wrote. But it can also mean other things. It can mean to happen: "There is going to *be* a parade." It can mean to occupy space: "The cake *is* on the table." It can mean to remain or continue as before: "Let it *be*. Let it be. Let be. Let it be. Speaking words of wisdom, let it be."

Now, watch this: *being* can be either a verb or a noun. We use it as a verb when we say, "She is *being* very sweet." We use it as a noun when we say, "She is a human *being*." But (and this is important for where this chapter is going), the noun is not very far removed from the verb. When we say, "She is a human being," we are using the noun, but we are implying the verb - she is a human be-ing. Her very be-ing, her very act of existing, the nature of her existence, is human. A being is something that exists, usually a living thing, and when we capitalize it we are usually referring to God: Being.

Is God A Being?

The problem is, when we start talking about God, about the One who cannot accurately be talked about, our finite words do a poor job of describing the Infinite One. He transcends all language, thought, and comprehension. He is so completely other that all our words and ideas fail. Still, we must use our words and ideas, finite though they are, in an attempt to discuss God, because they are the only words and ideas we are capable of using.

There was a writer in the early church who spent a lot of time communicating that God is simply above and beyond all our imagining and all our talk. Pseudo-Dionysius the Areopagite (no one knows his real name) was an early 6th century Eastern Christian (most likely Syrian) who wrote in his book *On The Divine Names* that we have to use words and names to talk about God, but that all our words and names fall short of describing the reality of who God is. So we say he is a spirit, but he is beyond spirit. We say that he is one, but he is beyond number. We say that he is the "highest being," but he is beyond being. God is, in short, transcendent. Transcendence means to surpass empirical reality, and God is so *other*, so *above and beyond* that he surpasses all things, even the "things" of words and ideas.

The early Christian writer Origen wrote, "God is incomprehensible, and incapable of being measured. For whatever be the knowledge which we are able to obtain of God, either by reflection or perception, we must of necessity believe that he is by many degrees far better than what we perceive him to be."[5]

St. Gregory of Nyssa, writing in the 4th century, wrote, "But we, following the suggestions of Scripture, have learned that the divine nature is unnameable and unutterable. We say that every name, whether it has been invented from human usage or handed down from Scripture, is an interpretation of the things thought about divine nature and does not encompass the significance of the nature itself."[6]

The rather laborious and clunky (but beautiful, once you "get" it) 6th century *Athanasian Creed*, which is actually neither by Athanasius nor a creed, sums it up with this line: "As also there are not three

---

[5] Origen, *De Principiis*, 1.5.

[6] Gregory of Nyssa, *Concerning We Should Thing of Saying That There Are Not Three Gods to Ablabius,* in *The Trinitarian Controversy,* edited by William G. Rusch, Fortress Press, Philadelphia, 1980; p. 149.

uncreated nor three *incomprehensible*, but one uncreated and one *incomprehensible*."

So, we *say* that God is a "being," but being (noun or verb) is a rather limiting word to use of God. Paul Tillich was a 20th century theologian who got into hot water in some Protestant circles for suggesting something that the Orthodox Church has maintained for nearly two millennia: that God isn't *a* being (that would make him, on some level, just one of everything else: here a being, there a being, everywhere a being being), but that he is Being itself. When we refer to him as *a* being we automatically place him in a category that is a box too small. Everything *else* is a being (the very word implies process and change, be-*ing*), but God is Being itself. St. Paul said much the same thing when he quoted the Greek poet in Acts 17.28, "In him we live and move and have our being," and continued by saying that everything else springs from him who is the ground of all being, "for we are indeed his offspring."

When Moses met God in the burning bush, he asked him who he was and God replied, "I AM" (Exodus 3.14). Or if we can put it in Ebonics, "I BE." No "ing" to it at all, no change, no process, no different tomorrow than today. God *is* "isness." God simply IS. "I AM." Not, "I was," or "I will be," but the timeless and eternal and ever present "I AM." He is beyond being itself.

The Invisible God

Now, if God is truly transcendent (and he is), then he is, from our perspective (and from any perspective outside his own), completely and utterly unknowable. He is, in other words, "unsensable" to us. We can't see, touch, taste, hear, or feel him. He is beyond our senses, beyond our ability to discover, beyond our ability to even know that he exists.

The biblical shorthand for this is the word "invisible." Paul wrote, "To the King of the ages, immortal, *invisible*, the only God, be honor and glory forever and ever. Amen" (1 Timothy 1.17).

When Moses asked to see God, I AM said to him, "No man can see God and live" (Exodus 33.20). John writes, "No man has seen God *at any time*" (John 1.18). Paul tells us that God "alone has immortality, who dwells in unapproachable light, whom no one has *ever* seen or *can* see" (1 Timothy 6.16).

Get it? No one ever has seen God. No one can see God. No one ever will see God. God is invisible. God transcends all our senses and comprehension.

And yet. And yet! People saw God!

Seeing God

We have just gone to great lengths to show from Scripture and theology that

God is unseeable. But now, from those same Scriptures and theology, we discover that people did indeed see God. Just three examples (there are many more):

In Genesis we read the story of Abraham's concubine Hagar, who bore to him his son Ishmael. After Abraham's wife Sarah got her dander up and insisted that the mother and child be cast out, Hagar found herself and her son in the desert in dire straits, and there encountered the Angel of the Lord, who told her to go back to Sarah and submit herself. After the Angel of the Lord departed, Genesis tells us, "So she called the name of the Lord who spoke to her, 'You are a God of seeing,' for she said, 'Truly *here have I seen him* who looks after me'" (Genesis 16.13).

Also in Genesis, Jacob encountered a mysterious being with whom he wrestled. After the wrestling match, this being gave him a new name - Israel. It really is worth reading the whole story, but pay attention to the closing words:

And Jacob was left alone. And a man wrestled with him until the breaking of the day. When the man saw that he did not prevail against Jacob, he touched his hip socket, and Jacob's hip was put out of joint as he wrestled with him. Then he said, "Let me go, for the day has broken." But Jacob said, "I will not let you go unless you bless me." And he said to him, "What is your name?" And he said, "Jacob." Then he said, "Your name shall no longer be called Jacob, but Israel, for *you have striven with God* and with men, and have prevailed." Then Jacob asked him, "Please tell me your name." But he said, "Why is it that you ask my name?" And there he blessed him. So Jacob called the name of the place Peniel, saying, "*For I have seen God face to face, and yet my life has been delivered*" (Genesis 32.24-30).

The third encounter is between God and Moses, the very man to whom God said, "No man can see me and live," and even in the *very same chapter*. Before the tabernacle was built (that kind of portable, traveling pre-Temple structure), Moses used to pitch a tent where he would encounter God. It was called "the Tent of Meeting" and he always pitched it a good distance away from the hubbub of community life. When he would go to the tent, the "cloud of glory" would park at the entrance, and God would go in and talk to Moses: "Thus the Lord used to speak to Moses *face to face, as a man speaks to his friend*" (Exodus 33.11).

There are obviously many other incidents of men and women in the Old Testament encountering, even *seeing*, the unseeable God. Adam, Abraham, Joshua, the prophets, and perhaps my favorite, Samson's mother, Mrs. Manoah (I know, I know, I said I would give three examples, but this fourth is just too good to pass up). The Angel of the Lord made several visits to Mrs. Manoah (and later to her husband) telling her that she would bear a son who would "save Israel from the hand of the Philistines." When Manoah himself finally encountered this person, he asked his name, to which the Angel of the Lord replied, "Why do you ask my name, seeing it is wonderful?" After the being disappeared (splendidly, I might add, stepping into the giant flame at an altar, not unlike God stepping into the pillar of fire when he was finished talking to Moses), Manoah said, ""We shall surely die, for *we have seen God*" (Judges 13.22). Of course they didn't die, and she went on to give birth to Samson, who saved Israel from the Philistines.

God's Self-Revelation

How can this be? It doesn't seem to add up. On the one hand God is invisible, unseeable, transcendent, beyond our ability to actually encounter, and on the other hand he's showing up all over the place in the Old Testament and people are seeing him and talking to him and hearing him talk back. How is it that this unknowable/unseeable/untouchable God is known and seen and touched?

The very fact that we believe or know that God exists at all is the result of what is called his *self-revelation*. The unknowable/unseeable/untouchable God has chosen of his own volition to make himself known and seen and touched. Now, this next part is very important: this self-revelation isn't the imparting of information, it is the imparting of the reality of God himself.

There are two words in the New Testament which refer to this revelation, *apocalypses*, which means unveiling or disclosing, and *phanerōsis*, which means exhibiting, manifesting, or expressing.[7] God unveils himself. He manifests himself. He reveals what was previously unrevealed. He exhibits what had not been exhibited before. And so, his self-revelation is a *progressive* thing. God doesn't fully reveal himself to Abraham or Moses. These people got glimpses of God, brief gazes, momentary encounters. The full revelation

7 Oden, Thomas, *The Living God*, Peabody, MA, Prince Press, 1998, p. 17.

comes later (but more about that later in the book).

This revelation of God is not a product of human discovery. This is where science and faith part ways. Science is about humans discovering reality, understanding empirical reality. Revelation is about the Undiscoverable One making himself known. This revelation from God has been understood as happening on two levels.

General (or common) revelation is the revelation to humans that God *is*, that he *exists*. Paul describes this kind of revelation when he writes, "For his invisible attributes, namely, his eternal power and divine nature, have been clearly perceived, ever since the creation of the world, in the things that have been made" (Romans 1.20). The heart of the human knows, even by the existence of creation itself (and particularly by the framework of his own being), that there is a creator. The scientist may not be able to find God through science (science simply does not address the existence of God, hence the use of science as an argument *against* the existence of God is a false argument), but God's fingerprints are all over the map of the universe. God can and does reveal himself anytime, anywhere, in any way it so pleases him.

   Special (or particular) revelation occurs when this God, who makes himself known generally in creation itself, chooses to make himself *particularly* known in a specific place and time, and to a particular person or people. Thomas Oden writes, "There remains a 'scandal of particularity' in all historical revelation. If God is to become known in history, then that must occur at some time and some place. It cannot occur at every time and in every place. The history of salvation is about those particular times and places and events."[8]

   God chose to reveal himself *more fully* in the history of and to the people of Israel

---

[8] *ibid*, p. 20.

- Abraham, Jacob, Moses, Miriam, Joshua, Hannah, Manoah and his wife, the Prophets, the Apostles - and through them to all of Israel. But as already stated, even that revelation was progressive. God did not reveal his fulness all at once, but as Hebrews tells us, "at many times and in many ways" (J.B. Phillips offers a masterful paraphrase of this text: "in bits and pieces."). And, although this is putting the cart before the horse, that revelation arrives in fulness through the incarnation of Jesus Christ - "but in these last days he has spoken to us by his Son, whom he appointed the heir of all things, through whom also he created the world. He is the radiance of the glory of God and the exact imprint of his nature, and he upholds the universe by the word of his power" (Hebrews 1.2,3).

Chapter Four

The Word of the Lord

Most of the time when modern Christians say, "The Word of God," they are referring to the Bible. That's all well and good, but when the Bible itself (both Old and New Testaments) refer to the Word of God it isn't making a self-referential statement. For example, when we read in Hebrews 4.12 that, "the word of God is living and active, sharper than any two-edged sword, piercing to the division of soul and of spirit, of joints and of marrow, and discerning the thoughts and intentions of the heart," we are making a significant mistake if we think the writer is referring to Scripture. The phrase meant something different to the Apostles and those who came before them, and its roots go all the way back to the first chapter of Genesis.

OK. Time for a joke. An old drunk was walking home from the bar late one night and decided to take a shortcut through the cemetery. In his condition and in the dark, he fell into an open, freshly dug grave. He spent a about an hour trying to climb out but kept falling back to the floor of the grave and he finally resigned himself to curl up in the corner, spend the night there, and wait for help in the morning. A little later another drunk made the same mistake. For about ten minutes he feverishly tried to climb his way out. From the pitch black corner the first drunk said, "You'll never get out of here."

But he did.

Our speaking is a revelation of our presence.

The Word in Creation

The very first self-revelation of the unknowable/unseeable/untouchable God was when he spoke. The first time we *see* God, the first time he makes himself known, is when he *says* something, and that something was, "Let there be light." Ten times in the first chapter of the Bible we read, "And God said…" God's *Word* and God's *Being* cannot be separated. Karl Barth wrote, "God's word is God himself in revelation."[9]

According to Scripture, God's Word *is* the power that brought about the universe. Genesis records that "God said..," but the Psalmist penned, "By *the word of the Lord* the heavens were made, And by the breath of His mouth all their host" (33.6). "The word of Yahweh is a creative agent, and it is fulfilled in the visible creation that results from it."[10]

---

[9] Barth, Karl, *Church Dogmatics*, Volume 1; Edinburg, T & T Clark, 1960; p. 339.

[10] Fortman, Edmund J., *The Triune God*, Grand Rapids, Baker, 1972, p. 4.

It is important to see that behind the divine speaking is divine power and authority. The Word of God comes forth from the inner depths of the unknowable/unseeable/untouchable God - from the Father - and carries with it the power of God to accomplish God's will and purpose. So, through the prophet Isaiah God can say, "so shall *my word* be that goes out from my mouth; it shall not return to me empty, but it shall accomplish that which I purpose, and shall succeed in the thing for which I sent it" (Isaiah 55.11).

So, creation itself is the result of the transcendent God manifesting himself through his Word, and in making himself known he creates out of nothing (except the power of his Word) this magnificent "other than him" that we call the universe and everything in it.

The Prophets

92 times in the Old Testament we find the phrase, "the Word of the Lord came to…" The first use of the phrase is in Genesis 15.1: "After these things *the word of the Lord* came to Abram in a vision, saying,'Do not fear, Abram, I am a shield to you; Your reward shall be very great.'" God, the Word of God, came to Abraham. God spoke, and revealed himself. God's Word is God himself in revelation. Let's take a quick romp through the Old Testament and see how the phrase is used.

It is used twice in Genesis (15.1,4), then the rest of the Pentateuch (the first five books of the Bible, the "Books of Moses") do not use the phrase in this way. But when we reach the historical books, when the office of the prophet reaches its ascendancy, it appears again in a stronger way. I am going to list eight examples. The tendency people have when they come to a list of Scriptures in a theology book is to just skim over them and not really pay attention. I am begging you to read them and think about them. See what they are saying.

- 1 Samuel 3.2: And the Lord appeared again at Shiloh, for the Lord revealed himself to Samuel at Shiloh by *the word of the Lord*.

- 1 Samuel 15.10: *The word of the Lord* came to Samuel…

- 2 Samuel 7.4: But that same night *the word of the Lord* came to Nathan…

- 2 Samuel 24.11: And when David arose in the morning, *the word of the Lord* came to the prophet Gad, David's seer…

- 1 Kings 6.11: Now *the word of the Lord* came to Solomon…

- 1 Kings 13.20: And as they sat at the table, *the word of the Lord* came to the prophet who had brought him back.

- 1 Kings 16.1: And *the word of the Lord* came to Jehu the son of Hanani against Baasha.

- 1 Kings 18.1: After many days the word of the Lord came to Elijah, in the third year, saying, "Go, show yourself to Ahab, and I will send rain upon the earth."

- 1 Chronicles 17.3: But that same night *the word of the Lord* came to Nathan…

In every instance, God *himself* comes to someone through the Word of the Lord. God reveals himself through his Word. His Word *is* his revelation, *is* him.

The Wisdom books use the phrase sparingly (we have already seen Psalm 33.6: "By *the word of the Lord* the heavens were made, and by the breath of his mouth all their host."), then the phrase goes full steam in the writings of the prophets, where it became the imprimatur of God stamped onto the ministry or the prophetic utterance of the various prophets. Notice, in the following list, how many of the prophetic books actually begin with the phrase.

- Isaiah 38.4: Then *the word of the Lord* came to Isaiah...

- Jeremiah 1.11: And *the word of the Lord* came to me, saying, "Jeremiah, what do you see?" And I said, "I see an almond branch."

- Ezekiel 1.3: *the word of the Lord* came to Ezekiel the priest, the son of Buzi, in the land of the Chaldeans by the Chebar canal, and the hand of the Lord was upon him there.

- Ezekiel makes use of it more than anyone - fifty times he says, "The *word of the Lord* came to me."

- Joel 1.1: *The word of the Lord* that came to Joel, the son of Pethuel...

- Jonah 1.1: Now *the word of the Lord* came to Jonah the son of Amittai…

- Micah 1.1: *The word of the Lord* that came to Micah of Moresheth…

- Zephaniah 1.1: *The word of the Lord* that came to Zephaniah the son of Cushi…

- Zechariah 1.1: In the eighth month, in the second year of Darius, *the word of the Lord* came to the prophet Zechariah…

- Malachi 1.1: The oracle of *the word of the Lord* to Israel by Malachi…

It becomes clear that the primary phrase of revelation in the Old Testament is, "the Word of the Lord came to…" When the Word of the Lord comes to someone, it is God himself coming to someone. God's Word is his revelation. The Word of the Lord *is* the Lord!

The Logos

When the Jewish world started interacting with the Greek world, and when more Jews spoke Greek than spoke Hebrew or Aramaic, the Scriptures were for the first time translated into the Greek language. Called the *Septuagint* (*LXX* for an abbreviation), it was translated by Jewish scholars in Alexandria, Egypt, and by the time of Christ and the Apostles had become the commonly used version (every Old Testament quote found in the New Testament is from the *LXX*). The *LXX* uses the Greek word *logos* for "word," and it also carries with it a long and complex history from the world of Greek philosophy. *Logos* means "word," "not in the grammatical sense, but…a word which, uttered by a living voice, embodies a conception of idea."[11]

At the time when Jesus was a boy growing up in Egypt, there lived a brilliant

---

[11] Thayer, Joseph Henry, *Greek-English Lexicon of the New Testament*, Grand Rapids, Zondervan, 1974, p. 358.

Jewish philosopher named Philo who attempted to unite the Jewish religion and Greek philosophy (one has to at least wonder if the little boy Jesus ever met the wise old philosopher). He found that this idea of "the Word" was common to both traditions, and spent a lot of his time building a case that the Greeks and Jews were pointing to the same thing. Philo saw the *logos* as a kind of mediating figure which comes from God, and which brings the transcendent (unknowable/unseeable/untouchable) God close to his creation. In other words, in the *logos*, God becomes immanent. In an odd twist (remember, this is *before* the New Testament was written), Philo also sees the *logos* as one who represents all of humanity as a high priest and advocate before the transcendent God. The *logos*, for Philo (and because of him, for much of the Jewish thinking world), "is the sum and locus of God's creative power, and as such it orders and governs the visible world."[12]

---

12 Kittel, v 4, p. 89.

So through Philo, at precisely the time that Christ was born, the Jewish scholars were seeing the Word of the Lord through slightly adjusted lenses, and recognizing that this Word who kept showing up in the Old Testament writings was a mediating, immanent presence of God himself.

The Gospel of John

There are four Gospels in the Bible. The first three are very similar, and called the Synoptic ("with the same eye") Gospels. The fourth, the Gospel of John, is different from the rest and has a decidedly more philosophical and theological feel to it. Whereas the other Gospels begin with the birth of Jesus, John lays hold of Philo's ideas, of Greek thought, of Jewish theology, and begins his Gospel with the famous phrase, "In the beginning was the Word (*logos*), and the Word was with God, and the Word was God."

Every well schooled Greek or Jew who read these words would instantly identify them with the *logos* of Greek philosophy and of Philo, and would immediately associate these words with the Old Testament "the Word of the Lord" who brought the world into existence and spoke to the Prophets. So far, so good. John isn't saying anything in this verse that is different than Philo. The Word was in the beginning. The Word was alongside God (shall we say coming forth from God). The Word *was* God! But then, in verse 14, John blows the lid off the philosophical/theological can: "And the Word *became flesh* and dwelt among us, and we have seen his glory, glory as of the only Son from the Father, full of grace and truth." God became human! The baby who's birth story is so beautifully told in the Gospel of Luke is the Word of God himself. God the Son, who reveals the glory of God to us. In his delightful book, *God Came Near*, Max Lucado offers 25 questions he would like to ask the Virgin Mary. The best one is the last one: "Did you ever think, That's God eating my soup?"

After the first chapter of John, the New Testament never again refers to Jesus as the Word until the end of Revelation, where we read, "And He is clothed with a robe dipped in blood; and His name is called The Word of God" (19.13).

The early leaders of the Church laid hold of this concept of the Word of God, the *logos*, and made much use of it. Justin Martyr (a Syrian Christian who was martyred in 165) wrote, "Since God is transcendent, the *logos* bridges the abyss between God and man."[13] St. Basil the Great (the bishop of Caesarea who died in 379) tells us that the Son is called the Word, "so that it be clear that he proceeded from the mind [of God]...because he is the image of his generator, *showing in himself the entire generator*."[14] Gregory of Nazianzus (who's thinking was so formative for the development of Trinitarian doctrine) wrote that the Son is called the Word, "because

---

[13] Justin Martyr, *Apologia*, 32.8

[14] Basil of Caesarea, *Homilies*, 16.3.

he is related to the Father as word to mind…because of the union, and of his declaratory function…the Son is a concise demonstration and easy setting forth of the Father's nature."[15]

Paul Tillich wrote, "*Logos* is the principle of the self-manifestation of God… Therefore, whenever God appears, either to himself or to others outside himself, it is the *Logos* which appears."[16]

The Word is the bringing forth of the mind. We think something, but until we articulate it, it remains invisible and unknowable, internalized. The Word of the Lord, that is, God the Son, is the bringing forth of the "inner God," that is, God the Father. The Word is the revelation of God himself. God, making himself known. God the Father reveals himself *only* through God the Son.

---

[15] Gregory of Nazianzus, *Orations*, 30.20.

[16] Tillich, Paul, *A History of Christian Thought*, New York, Simon and Schuster, p. 30.

Chapter Five

Two More Unveilings

There are angels all over the place in both testaments of the Bible. Abraham encounters them. So does Moses. So does Jacob, Isaiah, Ezekiel, Tobit, Daniel, Elijah, Sarah, Elisha, Lot, Joseph, Peter, Paul, and Mary. There are your every day run of the mill angels who don't even get named and there are archangels like Gabriel and Michael and Raphael, but there is one "angel" who merits a closer look. He's not just *any* angel of the Lord, he is *the* Angel of the Lord.

The Angel of the Lord

In the Old Testament a certain mysterious figure shows up at pivotal moments in the history of Israel, and although he *speaks* for God like other angels, there is something significantly different about him and about how people respond to him. If someone is giving the Scriptures just a quick read through, they might completely miss who this figure is, but close inspection reveals a major surprise.

In Genesis we find the story of Abraham's concubine Hagar. We have already visited her story in Chapter Three, where we discovered that, "she called the name of the Lord who spoke to her, 'You are a God of seeing,' for she said, 'Truly *here have I seen him* who looks after me'" (Genesis 16.13). The transcendent Lord spoke to her and appeared to her. Hagar saw the unseeable God. But now, let us revisit the tale and give closer attention to what happened. She and her son Ishmael are in the wilderness, fleeing the house of Abraham and Sarah, when, *"the angel of the Lord* found her by a spring of water in the wilderness"* (v. 7). This heavenly being speaks to her and instructs her to go back to Abraham's house and submit to Sarah, then he says, "I will surely multiply your offspring so that they cannot be numbered for multitude" (v. 11). Did you notice? *"I* will multiply your offspring." The Angel of the Lord is speaking in the first person about what God will do. He doesn't say, "God will multiply your offspring," he says, *"I* will multiply your offspring." After the encounter Hagar, "called the name of the Lord who spoke to her, 'You are a God of seeing…'" Who spoke to Hagar? The Angel of the Lord, or the Lord himself? The answer, of course, is yes.

Two chapters later, Abraham is dwelling in his tent when three men come walking up. The story begins, "And the Lord appeared to him by the oaks of Mamre, as he sat at the door of his tent in the heat of the day. He lifted up his eyes and looked, and behold, three men were standing in front of him" (Genesis 18.1,2). Three men come walking up to Abraham. One of them is the Lord. In verse 16 two of them set out for Sodom, and we are told in 19.1 that these two "men" were actually angels, who came to rescue Lot and his family from the impending doom of Sodom.

OK. Got the picture? Three men approach Abraham. One of them is the Lord. Two of them are angels who go on to Sodom. Then in verse 22 we are told, "the Lord had stayed with Abraham: So the men turned from there and went toward Sodom, but Abraham still stood before the Lord." Here is, again, a case of God himself showing up in some kind of angelic/humanlike form and making himself known.

Four chapters later, in Genesis 22, God tells Abraham to offer Isaac as a sacrifice. Abraham is obedient, goes to Mount Moriah, builds an altar, lays Isaac on it, and is about to kill him when the

Angel of the Lord calls to him and tells him not to lay a hand on Isaac. Then we read,

> "And *the angel of the Lord* called to Abraham a second time from heaven and said, 'By *myself* I have sworn, declares the Lord, because you have done this and have not withheld your son, your only son, I will surely bless you, and I will surely multiply your offspring as the stars of heaven and as the sand that is on the seashore.'" (Genesis 22.16,17).

Once again, the Angel of the Lord is the Lord, revealing himself to Abraham.

Five hundred years later Moses is in the wilderness tending sheep when he sees a bush burning but not burning up. In the old Sunday School flannelgraph pictures, Moses with his white robe and staff is standing staring at a little bush enveloped by fire, and we were told this is how God appeared to Moses. But a closer look at the text reveals something different:

And *the angel of the Lord* appeared to him in a flame of fire out of the midst of a bush. He looked, and behold, the bush was burning, yet it was not consumed. And Moses said, "I will turn aside to see this great sight, why the bush is not burned." When *the Lord* saw that he turned aside to see, *God* called to him out of the bush, "Moses, Moses!" And he said, "Here I am" (Exodus 3.2-4).

The fire wasn't God. God was *in* the fire. The Angel of the Lord was *in* the fire. The fire was a kind of vehicle or temporary abode in which the Angel of the Lord resided (in the same way, later in Exodus, the pillar of fire that traveled with the people of Israel as they made their way through the desert is a kind of vehicle in which the Lord dwelled). Then the Angel of the Lord says to Moses, "I am the God of your father, the God of Abraham, the God of Isaac, and the God of Jacob." And Moses hid his face, for *he was afraid to look at God*" (v. 6).

A few generations later, in the book of Judges, the cowardly Gideon was hiding out from the enemy when, "*the angel of the Lord* appeared to him and said to him, 'The Lord is with you, O mighty man of valor'" (Judges 6.12). After a lengthy encounter which included Gideon cooking supper and the Lord touching it with a staff and the whole thing bursting into flames, "Gideon perceived that he was *the angel of the Lord*. And Gideon said, 'Alas, O Lord God! For now *I have seen the angel of the Lord face to face*.' But the Lord said to him, "Peace be to you. Do not fear; you shall not die" (vs. 22,23). Gideon encountered the Angel of the Lord. That is to say, Gideon encountered God himself.

Just one more example. Remember back in Chapter Three when we learned about Mrs. Manoah, the mother of Samson? Remember her and her husband seeing God and Manoah saying, "We shall surely die, for we have seen the Lord"? Now, take half a minute and read the details in context:

And the *angel of the Lord* said to him,
"Why do you ask my name, seeing it
is wonderful?" So Manoah took the
young goat with the grain offering,
and offered it on the rock to the
Lord, to the one who works
wonders, and Manoah and his wife
were watching. And when the flame
went up toward heaven from the
altar, *the angel of the Lord* went up in
the flame of the altar. Now Manoah
and his wife were watching, and they
fell on their faces to the ground.

The angel of the Lord appeared no
more to Manoah and to his wife.
Then Manoah knew that he was *the
angel of the Lord*. And Manoah said to
his wife, "We shall surely die, for *we
have seen God*." But his wife said to
him, "If the Lord had meant to kill
us, he would not have accepted a
burnt offering and a grain offering at
our hands, or shown us all these
things, or now announced to us such
things as these." And the woman
bore a son and called his name

Samson. And the young man grew,
and the Lord blessed him (Judges
13.18-24).

The Angel of the Lord appeared to
Manoah and his wife. And they saw God.
The Angel of the Lord is God himself.

The Glory of the Lord

Another phrase used in the Old
Testament to denote God himself making
himself seen and known is "the glory of the
Lord." For example, in Exodus we read,

So Moses and Aaron said to all the
people of Israel, "At evening you
shall know that it was the Lord who
brought you out of the land of
Egypt, and in the morning you shall
see *the glory of the Lord*, because he
has heard your grumbling against
the Lord. For what are we, that you
grumble against us?"...And as soon
as Aaron spoke to the whole
congregation of the people of Israel,

they looked toward the wilderness, and behold, *the glory of the Lord* appeared in the cloud (Exodus 16.6-10).

Notice that the cloud was not the glory of the Lord. The glory of the lord appeared *in* the cloud. The cloud was a kind of vehicle that God rode around in. In Exodus 40.34 the vehicle pulls up to the Tabernacle, parks, and God gets out: "Then the cloud covered the tent of meeting, and *the glory of the Lord* filled the tabernacle," just like he used to before the Tabernacle was built and the cloud would park at the entrance of the tent of meeting and the Lord would go in and speak with Moses "face to face" (cf. Ex. 33.9-11).

When we think of the word glory we usually think of brilliant light or some numinous and nebulous glow, but the Hebrew word *kabowde* literally means "that which can be weighed." In other words, something tangible; something with physicality; something that was touchable, seeable, hearable. Later it came to mean wealth. A king of great glory was a man who had a lot of stuff that could be weighed - gold and silver and precious jewels. But when we read the phrase "the glory of the Lord" we ought to think of it as the transcendent God, the unknowable/unseeable/untouchable Lord, making himself immanent, making himself known and seen and touched.

Ezekiel actually describes precisely what this glory looked like, and what he saw in his heavenly vision is startling:

> And above the expanse over their heads there was the likeness of a throne, in appearance like sapphire; and seated above the likeness of a throne was *a likeness with a human appearance*. And upward from what had the appearance of his waist I saw as it were gleaming metal, like the appearance of fire enclosed all around. And downward from what had the appearance of his waist I saw as it were the appearance of fire, and there was brightness around

him. Like the appearance of the bow that is in the cloud on the day of rain, so was the appearance of the brightness all around. Such was the appearance of the likeness of *the glory of the Lord*. And when I saw it, I fell on my face, and I heard the voice of one speaking (Ezekiel 1.26-28).

"With a human appearance" - the glory of the Lord, the physical tangibility of God, was seen by Ezekiel to be in the form of a man! We can't leave the subject without pointing out that the prophet Isaiah, when he describes the coming of the Messiah, Jesus, writes, "And *the glory of the Lord* shall be revealed, and all flesh shall see it together, for the mouth of the Lord has spoken" (Isaiah 42.8). When the writer of Hebrews describes Jesus he says, "He is *the radiance of the glory of God* and *the exact imprint of his nature*, and he upholds the universe by the word of his power" (Hebrews 1.3).

The glory of the Lord is not some aura, some glow, some brilliance, it is the manifest presence of the One True God himself, made tangible to his people, the unseeable making himself seen.

The Word of God, the Angel of the Lord, and the Glory of the Lord - these are all the same thing: the self-revelation of the transcendent God. Another phrase for this same revelation, and one that encompasses and supersedes all these other designations, is *the Son of God*. Or, *God the Son*.

Chapter Six

God the Son

There once was a priest named Arius who was a really gifted songwriter. He was also a skilled preacher. His sermons were notable, but his songs spread like wildfire. He was born about 250 years after Christ in what is now Libya, studied in Antioch, and was a priest in Alexandria, Egypt. If it weren't for him, we wouldn't have the Nicene Creed, and he holds the distinction, according to tradition, of being the only guy ever smacked in the face by Santa Claus.

The problem was, Arius was an incredibly influential and popular heretic. He taught and sang that, "there was a time when the Son was not." His teachings were like an unstoppable plague and were so influential that the Church throughout the entire known world was thrown in to confusion and uproar. Finally, in 325 a council of church leaders from all over the world was convened in Nicea, a small city outside Constantinople (now Istanbul) to deal with the matter. It was there, according to tradition, that as Arius took the floor and began to argue that Jesus was *not* the One True God come in the flesh, St. Nicholas (the bishop of Myra) walked up and punched him in the face.

A Time When The Son Was Not

What Arius was arguing was that God the Father has existed from before time and forever, but that he begat the Son at some point in pre-history. In other words, the Son was a creation of the Father, was not of the same "stuff" as the

Father, and was therefore not *really* God. There was a time when the Son was not.

A young deacon named Athanasius, also from Alexandria, was at the council to assist his bishop and was the intellectual voice who won the day against Arius. Arius was so influential that Saint Jerome wrote, "the whole world groaned and was amazed to find itself Arian." Someone told Athanasius that the whole world was against him, to which he replied, "Then it is Athanasius against the world!" But upon close inspection, Arius' teachings fell apart, and Athanasius' solid, biblical, logical, and consistent argument won the day. Of the 318 bishops present, only two refused to sign the freshly written Nicene Creed.

There is a line in the creed which says that Jesus Christ is "the *only* begotten Son of God, *eternally* begotten of the Father, God of God, Light of Light, Very God of Very God, begotten, not made, *being of one substance* with the Father..." Only twenty or so words long, it remains to this day the most powerful and succinct setting forth of how Christians understand the relationship between God the Father and God the Son.

Only And Eternally Begotten

No one uses the word begotten anymore in common speech. When was the last time you heard someone say, "Jimmy was begotten by his father Sammy?" We tend to equate begotten with born, but the two words are completely different. The Greek word translated begotten is *ginomai*, and it means *brought forth* (the King James Version actually translates *ginomai* as "published" in Acts 10.37). A mother gives birth. A father begets. What the creed is saying is that the Son is the *only* "bringing forth" of the Father, and that this bringing forth has no beginning. Within the nature of God, the Son is *eternally* brought forth from the Father. Read again the first lines from the Gospel of John and notice how it ties together all the things we have been thinking through:

In *the beginning* was the Word, and the Word was with God, and *the Word was God*. He was in the beginning with God…And the Word became flesh, and dwelt among us, and we saw His *glory*, glory as of the *only begotten from the Father*, full of grace and truth…*No one has seen God at any time*; the *only begotten God* who is in the bosom of the Father, He has explained Him" (John 1.1-2,14,18, NASB).

The Son was *born* to a woman, in history, in Bethlehem. But he is *eternally begotten* of the Father. When the Old Testament prophet Micah prophesied the birth of the Messiah, he is careful to point out that the Son doesn't *begin* in Bethlehem: "But you, O Bethlehem Ephrathah, who are too little to be among the clans of Judah, from you shall come forth for me one who is to be ruler in Israel, whose *coming forth* (*ginomai*; being begotten) is from of old, from ancient days" (Micah 5.2).

God the Son became flesh in the womb of the Virgin Mary. He was born in history in Bethlehem. But he is "brought forth, "begotten," "published," from the Father eternally. Gregory of Nazianzus wrote, "There was not when [God] was Wordless, or when he was not the Father."[17]

St. Ignatius of Antioch, trained and ordained by the Apostles themselves (and fed to the lions in the Colosseum in Rome), writing two hundred years before the Arian controversy, said it simply and well: "For there is one God who manifested Himself in Jesus Christ His Son, who is His Word proceeding from silence."[18]

The Son is the *only publishing* of the Father. He is the *constantly-being-published* expression of the invisible God!

---

[17] Gregory of Nazianzus, *Third Theological Oration (17)*, in Rusch, p. 143.

[18] Ignatius, *Letter to the Magnesians, 8.2.*

One Substance With The Father

My maternal grandfather, born in 1913, was a third grade educated farmer in Texas, but he spoke Greek. He didn't *know* he was speaking Greek, but he was. First, when he would call the cows to the barn he would yell, "Bossy, bossy, bossy! Heeeere, bossy!" Bossy is just a corruption of *bous*, the Greek word for cow. My grandpa's second use of Greek is much more theologically significant. When he wanted to express his lack of care or concern for something, he would say, "Well, I don't give one iota about that!" Iota is the Greek letter for *i*, and although he didn't know it, my grandfather was referencing the huge debate at the Council of Nicea over one tiny Greek letter in a word.

Homoousios and *homoiousios*. Two words, with two completely different meanings, only one tiny *i* apart. *Homoousios* means "the same substance" and *homoiousios* means "a similar substance." The Arians were arguing that the Son was kind of like the Father, made by the Father, and of a similar substance. The substance of the Father was pure deity. The substance of the son was related, similar, like, very close, but not identical to the substance of the Father. The orthodox side was saying, "No! The Son is precisely the same substance with the Father." Now, remember when we learned that the word holy means unique? Remember when we talked about God being singular, being One? When we speak of the substance of the Son being "one with" or "the same" as the substance of the Father, we don't mean to say that there are two (or three) batches of Divine Being that are the same stuff. We mean to say that there is One-Batch-Of-Divinity. One God: Father, Son, and Holy Spirit. The Son is, as the creed states, "God of God, Light of Light, Very God of Very God."

For centuries, I suppose, people have tried to use various analogies to explain this Trinity of persons in the Godhead, and all analogies fall short, but some of them are really terrible and do great damage. There is one that works better than the others, and it is actually the analogy used in the Bible, but almost never used today in helping us understand God.

Chapter Seven

God In Three Persons

Three peas in one pod. The shell, the yolk, and the yellow, but one egg. Steam, liquid, and solid, but all of it water. A father, a son, a husband, but one man. The skin, the meat, the seed, but one peach. A flame, a glow, and warmth, but one candle. All of these are analogies used to help explain the Trinity, and they are all terrible. Some of them are modalistic (showing God as simply taking on three different roles), some of them are tritheistic (showing God as three different substances), and some of them are downright silly. If we're going to think reasonably about the three persons of the Trinity, we have to come up with a better analogy, but first we have to deal with that confusing word, *persons*.

Person, Persona, Hypostasis

I'm giving you fair warning. This next section is totally confusing. Read it slowly and thoughtfully, then reread it, then reread it again.

When Athanasius was writing about God the Father, the Son, and the Holy Spirit he couldn't come up with a satisfactory word to describe the *distinctions* in the Godhead. He said there were three "somethings," but he wasn't comfortable with the word which ends up in English as *persons*.

When we use the word *person* today, we usually mean *individual*. But God is not three individuals. Karl Barth, probably the most significant Protestant theologian of the 20th century, wrote, "'Person' in the sense of the Church doctrine of the Trinity has nothing directly to do with 'personality'. Thus the meaning of the doctrine of the Trinity is not that there are three personalities in God. That would be the worst and most pointed expression of tritheism."[19]

The Latin word *persona*, first used to describe the Trinity by Tertullian early in the third century isn't much better. Originally it meant a mask worn by an actor on stage. One actor could play three different roles and still be the same actor. But this old definition of the word smacks of the heresy of modalism (that the Father, Son and Holy Spirit are just three different roles played by God), and so *persona* doesn't work well either.

The Greeks used the word *hypostasis*, and it is almost untranslatable into English or Latin. *Hypostasis* itself is problematic in that it *originally* meant substance, and was sometimes used interchangeably with *ousios* (remember *homoousios* and *homoiousios* -

---

19 Barth, p. 403.

the same substance vs. a similar substance?). It almost makes no sense to say we believe that God is one *ousios* but three *hypostases*. This comes close to saying we believe God is one substance but three substances. But words change in meaning over time, and *hypostasis* came to mean something akin to our word *existence*.[20] One possible way we could translate it is *realities*. God is one substance, but within that one substance there are three realities, three distinctions; maybe Athanasius was right, three *somethings*. Three *je ne sais quoi!*

But of course we will and should continue to use the word persons because we simply don't have another good word with which to replace it, and it has so settled into theology as to be a word that doesn't need to be jettisoned, just carefully defined. We believe that there is One God,

---

[20] The King James Version muddies the waters even more by translating *hypostasis* as both person and substance. In Hebrews 1.3, describing the Son, it reads, "Who being the brightness of his glory, and the express image of his *person*" but in Hebrews 11.1 it reads, "Now faith is the *substance* of things hoped for, the evidence of things not seen."

One Divine Being. But within God there are three distinctions. In other words, there is that which is of the Father that is not of the Son and the Spirit; there is that which is of the Son that is not of the Father and the Spirit. There is that which is of the Spirit that is not of the Father and the Son.

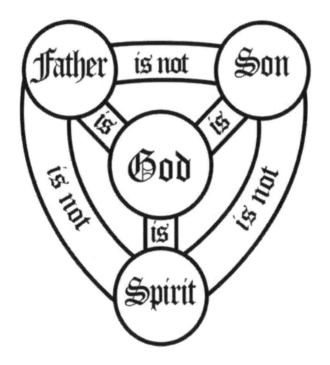

The Father begets, or "brings forth," or "publishes." The Son is the begotten, or brought forth, or published. The Spirit isn't begotten, but proceeds from the Father - the Spirit is, for lack of a better way of saying it, the begottenness itself. Barth said the Father is the Revealer, the Son is the Revealed, and the Spirit is the "Revealedness."[21]

Let me give you two examples of this, the first from the Bible and the second from liturgy. In the first chapter of the Gospel of Luke we find that Gabriel comes to the Virgin Mary with a message from God that she will conceive and bear a son who will be the Savior and will be called "the Son of the Most High" (v. 32). When Mary asked how this would happen, the angel said, "The Holy Spirit will come upon you, and the power of the Most High will overshadow you; therefore the child to be born will be called holy - the Son of God" (v. 35). Notice the process:

---

[21] Barth, p. 347.

1. The Father wills this to happen. He is the Sender, the Revealer, the Begetter.

2. The Spirit proceeds from the Father and overshadows Mary. The Spirit is the "power of the Most High." He is the "Revealedness" or "Begottenness."

3. The *result* is God the Son being born in the flesh; God made manifest; God published. The Son is the Revealed, the Begotten, the Published One.

There is a piece in the liturgy of Holy Communion called the *epiclesis,* or "calling down," in which the priest lays his hands on the bread and wine, and asks the Father to send the Holy Spirit upon them, and make them to be the Body and Blood of Christ. Again, note the process:

1. The Father is invoked, and sends the Spirit.

2. The Spirit proceeds from the Father and comes upon the Bread and Wine.

3. The result is the bread and wine become theBody and Blood of Christ. That is, God the Son is made manifest!

These distinctions of Revealer, Revealed and Revealedness, these differentiations, are within the very nature of God himself. It may be that the best way to understand this is to lay aside egg shells, ice cubes, and pea pods, and look to an analogy that is closer to God himself, one which we find in Scripture.

In His Own Image

In Genesis 1, when he finally got around to creating humanity, "God created man in his own image, in the image of God he created him; male and female he created them" (v. 27). Perhaps then, if we are attempting to wrestle with understanding the nature of God, we ought to look at something which is closer to his nature than, say, an egg. Using the analogy of a human, like all analogies, will fall terribly short of the mark, because God is so completely "other" that all our words and ideas fall short. But still, it does so happen that God himself said we were made in his image, and he never said that about ice cubes or candlesticks. So let's at least give it a shot. And we won't look at humanity in general, we will be very specific. Let's talk about *you*.

The Inner You: There is a you that only you know. There is this inner you, where all the thoughts and ideas happen, where emotions happen, where all the rest of you begins, and that inner you is known only to you. No one else, not your best friend, your spouse, your coworker, knows this inner you. This is you the revealer. In our analogy, this is God the Father. He is the "inner God," so to speak. No one else can see him or know him. He is known to himself and himself alone. But from him flows all else that is him.

The Outer You: There is, alongside the inner you, the outer you. Your physical make up, your personality, your voice, everything that makes up "you" as you are known to the world around you. The phone rings, and I pick up and hear your voice and know instantly it is you. I see you across the street and recognize you by the way you walk and call out your name. Your fingers type me an email and through those ten digits on your hands the inner you communicates through the outer you to me.

Now, the significant thing is, the *only* way anyone can get to know the inner you is through the outer you. I can't read your mind. I don't know your wants and wishes. But you can *reveal* your mind to me through talking to me with your mouth, or typing to me with your fingers, or winking at me with your eye, or slapping me with your hand. In our analogy, this is God the Son. The Son (from before time and forever, "eternally begotten") is the "outer God." The Son is the Revealed, the Revelation, the Begotten, the Published. He is the *only* begotten of the Father. When the Son became flesh in the person of Jesus, he said, "No one comes to the Father except through me" (John 14.6). Of course not! The only way I can get to the inner you is through the outer you. The only way any of us can get to the Father is through the Son. When Philip asked Jesus to show them the Father, Jesus said, "Have I been with you so long, and you still do not know me, Philip? Whoever has seen me has seen the Father" (John 14.9).

The obvious breakdown in this analogy is that you can be hypocritical or less than honest and show me something that isn't really you. You can say one thing ("Oh, that's a lovely leopard skin pill box hat you're wearing!"), and be thinking something completely different ("Oh, my! You look like such an idiot, I wonder how your head feels under something like that."). But with God, what you see is what you get. The Son is the "exact imprint of his nature" (Hebrews 1.3), the "image of the invisible God" (Colossians 1.15), and with God, "there is no variation or shadow due to change" (James 1.17).

The Influencing You: There is not only the inner you (the revealer), and the outer you (the revealed), there is also the influencing you, the you that impacts things and other people. You aren't even around but your husband says, "My wife would want me to help out that poor man with the broken down car on the side of the road." You aren't even around, but your wife holds up a jacket and says, "Doesn't this just *look like* him? I have to buy it while it's on sale. He'll love it!" You aren't even around, but your employee says, "I really need to get this painting done, because the boss says it needs to be finished by the end of the day." You aren't even around, but your teenage son says, "Well, I need to pick up my dirty clothes and clean my room, because that's what Mom would like." Well, OK, that last one was a little far fetched, but you get the idea. You have influence even when you aren't there. Here is where our analogy weakens, because there is a difference between God and you! God is never "not there." He is omnipresent. He is fully and completely there all the time. But in the analogy, this is the Holy Spirit, the "Revealedness" of God which goes forth from the Father; the Power of God who effects change; the breath of God which breathes out the Word from the Father, and which gives life to all.

Only One You: But of course, there aren't three of you walking around. There is only one you. And there aren't three Gods that form some kind of Divine Committee on Godness who sit around all day discussing what to create or sustain next. And there certainly aren't a Father and a Son who are on different sides of the argument regarding the salvation of the world, with the Father saying, "I really ought to whack them all," and the Son saying, "Aww, come on Dad, let me take their punishment instead." But I digress.[22] There is only One God; one substance; one Divine Nature: the Father, the Son, and the Holy Spirit.

Karl Barth wrote, "The content of revelation is *wholly* God. The point here is simply that God is not just half revealed or partly revealed...The revealed God and the hidden God are one and the same, and he is the total God, the Lord Sabaoth, beside whom there is no other."[23]

"I and the Father are one," Jesus said (John 10.30), and he meant more than just that they agree on things.

---

[22] But our understanding of the oneness of the nature of God does impact our understanding of how salvation works. See my *Salvation And How We Got It Wrong*, Denison, TX, Mayeux Press, 2013.

[23] Barth, Karl, *The Göttingen Dogmatics: Instruction in the Christian Religion,* Grand Rapids, Eerdmans, 1991, p. 103.

Chapter Eight

What If God Was One Of Us?

     I sat across the table from the young man discussing who Jesus is. He kept telling me there was no way Jesus was God himself. That could not be possible. Jesus was a man filled with the Holy Spirit. He was the Son of God. He was a prophet. He was our Savior. But I shouldn't even begin to try to convince him that Jesus was *God*.

     I know what you are thinking: I was chatting with a Mormon. Maybe one of Jehovah's Witnesses. Perhaps a Muslim.

Nope. I was chatting with a Christian. A Christian who had been raised devoutly in the Christian faith since birth. A Christian who was a pastor's son.

And he wasn't going through some rebellious streak. He wasn't dancing on the edge of apostasy. He was just telling me what he had always understood. He'd never heard it put to him in a clear, point-blank manner, that Jesus was "very God of very God."

Who is this Jesus? That has been the question from the start. The Apostles and the early Christians were quick to affirm that he was indeed God come in the flesh, but this caused all kinds of problems among the Jewish religious leaders of the day. As Christianity spread to the Gentile world the questions didn't stop. The first several centuries of theological wrangling centered around who Jesus was and how there could be One True God and yet Jesus could also be God. Various heresies tried to explain it away, often being polar opposites of one another, and as difficult as those times were, they helped the Church clarify the faith by saying, "No, *that* is not what we believe, but *this* is," giving rise to the saying that heresy precedes orthodoxy. This is where the creeds come from. This is where the early statements on the nature of God, Christ, and the Holy Spirit come from. So, who is this Jesus, born of a Virgin, into our world and our history?

The Word Made Flesh

We have already spent an entire chapter dealing with the Word (*logos*), but let us be reminded that John begins his gospel declaring, "In the beginning was the Word, and the Word was *with* God, and the Word *was* God" (John 1.1). That would have been an acceptable statement to the readers of the day, both Jew and Greek. Where eyebrows began to raise was when John went on to write, "And the Word *became flesh* and dwelt among us, and we have seen his glory, glory as of the only Son from the Father, full of grace and truth" (v. 14).

Jesus isn't *a* son of God, he is *the* Son of God. He is the *only* Son of God. He is God the Son. This unique and singular revelation of God, given various names in the Old Testament (the Word of the Lord, the Angel of the Lord, the Glory of the Lord, etc.) became flesh in the womb of a young virgin Jewish girl and was born into our history, forever joining *our* nature with the nature of *God*. Years before John wrote his gospel, the Apostle Paul quotes something that is close to being a creed when he wrote, "Great indeed, we confess, is the mystery of godliness: *He was manifested in the flesh*, vindicated by the Spirit, seen by angels, proclaimed among the nations, believed on in the world, taken up in glory" (1 Timothy 3.16).

Simply put, Jesus was exactly who the angel told Mary he would be: Immanuel, "God with us" (Matthew 1.23).

The Image of God

All throughout the Old Testament the people of Israel are forbidden from making an image of God. How could they, if God is invisible? The other nearby religions would make statues of things representing some attribute of God (God is strong, like a bull, so let's make a statue of a bull to portray God's strength), or representing their local tribal deity (Baal, Ashtorah, Molech, or whomever), but Israel was strictly forbidden from joining in that game.

In the Greek, Roman, and pagan worlds we have a different story. There are images of the gods all over the place. The Greeks had a very different concept of images than the Jews did, and believed that an image (the Greek word is *eikon,* from which we get *icon*) was actually connected to that which it portrayed. It somehow presented what it portrayed.

Another way to say it, an *eikon* was *an image in which the original is contained.*[24]

The Apostle Paul, as a well educated and well traveled Jew, could traverse the two cultures and speak as easily in the language of Greek philosophy as he could in the language of rabbinic Judaism. When he wrote to the culturally Greek Christians in Colossae in Asia Minor, he wrote of Jesus,

> *He is the image [eikon] of the invisible God*, the firstborn of all creation. For by him all things were created, in heaven and on earth, visible and invisible, whether thrones or dominions or rulers or authorities -

[24] "The peculiarity of the expression is related to that of the ancient concept, which does not limit image to a functional representation present to human sense but also thinks of it in terms of an emanation, of a revelation of the being with a substantial participation (μετοχή) in the object. Image is not to be understood as a magnitude which is alien to the reality and present only in the consciousness. It has a share in the reality. Indeed, it is the reality. Thus εἰκών does not imply a weakening or a feeble copy of something. It implies the illumination of its inner core and essence." (Kittel, Gerhard, TDNT, Volume 2, p. 389.)

all things were created through him and for him. And he is before all things, and in him all things hold together...*For in him all the fullness of God was pleased to dwell...* (Colossians 1.15-19).

This, according to Paul, is who Jesus is: the image of God which contains the original! The writer of Hebrews reinforces what Paul said in Colossians:

Long ago, at many times and in many ways, God spoke to our fathers by the prophets, but in these last days he has spoken to us by his Son, whom he appointed the heir of all things, through whom also he created the world. He is *the radiance of the glory of God* and *the exact imprint* of his nature, and he upholds the universe by the word of his power (Hebrews 1.1-3).

The Form of God

Morphe is another important Greek word which has also made its way into English (metamorphosis, morph, and in a very roundabout way even morphine), and it has nothing whatsoever to do with the *nature* of a thing, but with the *appearance* or *form* of a thing. When a caterpillar changes into a butterfly, when it goes through metamorphosis, it doesn't change who it is. It doesn't change its nature. It is still the same being. It changes how it looks. It changes form. With all this in mind, read what Paul wrote to the Christians in Philippi (another culturally Greek congregation):

> Have this mind among yourselves, which is yours in Christ Jesus, who, though he was in the *form* of God, did not count equality with God a thing to be grasped, but emptied himself, by taking the *form* of a servant, being born in the likeness of men. And being found in human *form*, he humbled himself by

becoming obedient to the point of
death, even death on a cross
(Philippians 2.5-8).

Now, think about what Paul said.
Jesus Christ, before he was ever born to
the Virgin, was in the *form* of God. He had
the appearance of God. Or to be more
precise, he *was* the appearance of God (he
was the Word, the Angel of the Lord, the
Glory of the Lord). Without changing
nature (he was still God; how can God stop
being God?), he changed *form*, and took on
the form of a human, a servant.

Who is Jesus? He is God come in
human form. But this doesn't mean that he
simply put on a "man costume" for thirty
three years, then laid it aside. In the person
of Jesus, God joined himself to humanity
forever ("he *became* flesh," John tells us).
Jesus is fully God and fully man. In one
person the two natures were joined
permanently. When Christ ascended, he
ascended as a human. A man (someone
who literally shares our DNA - we are all
his distant cousins) sits on the Throne of

God. When Paul described Jesus taking on the form of a human, he continued,

> Therefore God has highly exalted him and bestowed on him the name that is above every name, so that at the name of Jesus every knee should bow, in heaven and on earth and under the earth, and every tongue confess that Jesus Christ is Lord, to the glory of God the Father (Philippians 2.9-11).

The Chalcedonian Creed

In 451, to settle a dispute over the nature of Christ, another council was held in Chalcedon (like Nicea, also near Constantinople), and the clarifying statement that emerged is called the Chalcedonian Creed or the Chalcedonian Definition. It is rather complex, but in light of all we have learned, give it a careful reading:

Therefore, following the holy fathers, we all with one accord teach men to acknowledge one and the same Son, our Lord Jesus Christ, at once complete in Godhead and complete in manhood, truly God and truly man, consisting also of a reasonable soul and body; of one substance with the Father as regards his Godhead, and at the same time of one substance with us as regards his manhood; like us in all respects, apart from sin; as regards his Godhead, begotten of the Father before the ages, but yet as regards his manhood born, for us men and for our salvation, of Mary the Virgin, the God-bearer; one and the same Christ, Son, Lord, Only-begotten, recognized in two natures, without confusion, without change, without division, without separation; the distinction of natures being in no way annulled by the union, but rather the characteristics of each nature being preserved and coming together to form one person and subsistence, not as parted or separated into two persons, but one and the same Son and Only-begotten God the Word, Lord Jesus Christ; even as the prophets from earliest times spoke of him, and our Lord Jesus Christ himself taught us, and the creed of the fathers has handed down to us.

Who is Jesus? He is God. He is man. He is "one of us." He is the union of the Creator and his creation. In him is the reconciliation of God and humanity.

"We know what God looks like; God looks like Jesus. We know what God sounds like; God sounds like Jesus. We know how God acts; God acts like Jesus."[25]

---

[25] Kenneth Tanner, *How We Know God*, Sojourners, http://sojo.net/blogs/2013/04/24/how-we-know-god, 2013.

Chapter Nine

For Us And For Our Salvation

Why does it matter? Jesus was God. Big deal. So what?

St. Gregory of Nazianzus, the fourth century father so significant for thinking and writing about the Trinity, figured that the very first philosophical/theological question anyone asks themselves is, "How can I be saved?" All religions in one way or another are attempts to answer this question, and everyone (even people who don't believe in any religion or any god, and who would never use the word "sin") recognizes that something is wrong with the human condition. There is evil, there is fallenness, things are not as they should be or as we wish they could be.

So, if St. Gregory is right and if the first question we ask is about how we can be saved, then all other theology - our wrestling with who God is, with who Jesus is, with who we are, flows out from this primal question we have about how things can be made the way they ought to be.

Instead of developing a long chapter on soteriology (the study of salvation), I'm going to recommend you read another book I wrote on the subject,[26] I'm going to share three little articles I have already published in a blog, and I'm going to conclude with some theological reflections from the early church. First, the three blogposts.

---

[26] Myers, Kenneth, *Salvation And How We Got It Wrong*, Denison, TX, Mayeux Press, 2013.

Just Some Questions About Jesus Paying It All

Someone wrote about Good Friday that this is the day when "Jesus paid it all." I responded with the question, "*Who* did Jesus pay?" He responded,

> It was a legal transaction that allowed unholy humans to enter into fellowship a perfect God. As far as who, I would have to say, God. The Judge. Jesus paid our fine. To get more specific would be to get into intricacies of the Trinity I suppose. Jesus is the second person of the Trinity, but while on earth, received the wrath of the Father, the first person of the Trinity. But we know Jesus will come at a future date in judgment, read, wrath. So the short answer is, *Jesus* paid *God* the fine we were supposed to pay.

So I just asked a series of questions - food for thought:

1. Do the Father and the Son (aren't they one?) have different agendas? The Father insisting on being "paid" in order to forgive, the Son volunteering to pay? Isn't this, perhaps, a crack in the unity of the Trinity? Didn't God (the Father) so *love* the world that he sent his only Son?

2. Is forgiveness really forgiveness if a debt has to be paid first? Would it be true forgiveness for you to say to someone, "I'll forgive you, but first you have to pay"?

3. Jesus came to show us what God is like. God is like Jesus. Period. Jesus is the express image of the invisible God; he does nothing without seeing the Father do it first; the fulness of the Godhead was in Christ. Is God a forgiving God, or a bookkeeping God? What about all the parables Jesus gave to describe the forgiving nature of God and to teach us how to forgive in imitation of God himself? Did God "need" or "have to

have" a payment made, a penalty given, in order to forgive humanity?

4. You wrote, "It was a legal transaction that allowed unholy humans to enter into fellowship a perfect God." - Wasn't Jesus himself that "perfect God?" And yet, did he not have fellowship with us before his death? Did he not have fellowship with sinners (much to the scandal of the religious leaders)?

5. Is it possible that we (by we I don't mean all of Christianity, I mean particularly us Christians in the West who have inherited a soteriology from medieval theologians) have gotten wrong the whole point of Christ's incarnation, death and resurrection?

6. What if it wasn't about payment at all? What if it wasn't about penalty at all? What if it was about rescue, from the heart of a loving Father, through the action of the Son?

We Really Need A Different Story

Did the Father pour out his wrath on the Son in order to reconcile us to himself? That's pretty common thinking among American Christians of the Evangelical persuasion, but take a step back from it and look at it from a distance; it suddenly seems to be a grotesque image, and shows a disposition that, were we to see it in some human being, we would call "disturbed."

Here is the scene. We'll call the fellow Benny. Benny is the CEO of a big company, has a lot of land, a lot of money, and a lot of power. Benny has his entire workforce go on strike against him although he's done nothing but treat them fairly and beyond their expectations. His company is a mess, and he has to step in to try to salvage things, and he is now really ticked with all the people who got him into this fix to begin with.

Really ticked. Really, really ticked. So ticked. Benny's anger, his wrath, can't dissipate, he can't just go fishing for a day and get over it - it *has* to be vented. Someone is going to have to pay.

On the other hand, Benny is a nice guy, and he really doesn't want to have to take out his anger on everybody. He'd like to forgive and forget but that simply isn't an option for two reasons: first, his anger is real and he has to vent it *somewhere*, and two, what would everyone think if he just forgave them? He'd be seen as a pushover and no one would ever listen to a word he said after that.

So Benny comes up with a plan. He decides to take his own son, the incredibly kind and gentle Benny Jr., and in front of God and the whole world he is going to let go the full fury of all his pent up rage upon his boy. So Benny gets Junior (who willingly does what his daddy wants him to do) and chains him to a tree in front of corporate headquarters. Then he takes a lead pipe and beats the living daylights out of Junior. Over and over he pummels him until his son is a bloody pulp. All the people are standing at a distance, gasping in horror as Junior collapses to the ground but doesn't fall because his arms are chained to the limb above him. He dangles there. And Benny continues to whack him. Until. He. Dies.

But it had to be done. I mean, justice demanded that *someone* pay for strike down at the factory. Benny couldn't just forgive the workers. But he also couldn't take out his ire on them because he really cared for them - even loved them.

I said all that to say this: ***Benito is not a good person. Benny doesn't need appeasing. Benny needs therapy.***

✿ ✿ ✿ ✿ ✿ ✿ ✿ ✿ ✿

And yet, this is precisely the picture that many Christians paint of God. He poured out his wrath upon his own Son as the only remedy for dealing with our sins, the only way to reconcile us to himself.

When I argue against such an understanding some people think I'm some kind of heretic. Never mind that no one believed this kind of stuff for the first thousand years of Christianity, if you don't believe it now there's something wrong with you.

"But, the Bible is clear about the wrath of God," they say to me, "if Christ did not satisfy the Father's righteous wrath against sin, then either we cannot be forgiven or God cannot be just."

Well, I would argue that Christ *did* satisfy "the Father's righteous wrath against sin." But let me be careful and clear in this response:

God is wrathful toward sin. He hates it. Just like a surgeon is wrathful toward cancer and hates it, and cuts it out of the patient's body. And Christ, as a good spiritual surgeon, did satisfy God's demand that sin be removed and destroyed ("Behold, the Lamb of God, who *takes away* the sin of the world"). But God the Father did not pour out his wrath on the Son, he poured out his wrath on sin itself. And he is still doing so, and will continue to do so until it is obliterated from his creation.

❀ ❀ ❀ ❀ ❀ ❀ ❀ ❀

The whole Benny story is just wrongheaded. We need a different story. Maybe someone should write a new version, with Benny being the most wonderful guy in the whole world, and his factory being infiltrated by an evil man who deceives all the workers. They actually believe the things this evil man tells them but they become slaves, working for peanuts, miserable, with no hope of things ever changing. So Benny enlists the aid of his son…

I'll keep it short and tell you how it ends: his son raids the factory, gets pummeled by the bad guys and everyone actually assumes it was a failed cause, but he rallies and liberates the people, shows them the truth, and kicks the bad guy in the, ummm, derriere.

I hear they're making the story into a movie. It's going to star Bruce Willis. Yippee ki yay.

A Different Angle On That Whole Salvation Thing

Modern soteriology (the study of salvation) is in a mess, and the problem started with Augustine, who so incredibly influenced the whole of Western theology. It expands in later medieval times with Anselm's *Cur Deus Homo (Why God Became Man)*. Anselm, too, influenced the West. The Protestant Reformers took it even further, with their Anselmian/Augustinian base of understanding, and developed the whole Penal Substitutionary Atonement doctrine.

In short, the West tends to look at the whole salvation thing as juridical - mankind (through Adam, original sin, and "sinful nature") is conceived and born under the wrath of God - estranged from God, worthy only of damnation, and (here is the important point) *unable to pay God for their sin*. So God (who is disposed by necessity of his being to be *wrathful* toward fallen man) sends his Son to become incarnate, live and die as a sinless man, and *pay* (pay whom? Pay God!) for our sins in order for us to be forgiven. Forgiveness, then, isn't forgiveness as we are taught by Jesus to forgive (not looking for repayment), but forgiveness is only achieved through *someone* - an *innocent* someone - *paying God* on our behalf.

The question emerges, why is God's forgiveness something to be bought? Isn't forgiveness the *canceling* of sin/debt (consider the parables of Jesus on the subject)?

Forgiveness then becomes a very transactional thing. We sin, we pull the right lever (baptism, confession, or if you are Protestant, walking the aisle, kneeling by the side of your bed confessing your sins to

God, whatever), and God gives us a dose of forgiveness to cover us until the next time.

It's all about *how God sees us.*
Juridical. Courtroom decisions.
Bookkeeping. Balancing columns.

The patristic (and Eastern) model is more holistic: Adam sinned, and by his sin let sin and death into the world. The original mandate, "Don't eat from the tree or you will die," was not a threat, but a warning. It wasn't a threat of, "Don't eat from the tree or *I will kill you*," it was a warning of, "That tree is spiritually poison, don't eat from it, *it will kill you*." Sin enters the world, a kind of *spiritual disease*, and it gets passed on to all of us from Adam (the closest this view comes to Original Sin). But it isn't something in our *nature*, it's something we *have* (Read Romans 7 in light of this).

God's disposition toward us was not one of wrath, but love - "For God so *loved* the world that he sent his only begotten

Son…" - it was a rescue operation from the get go. The idea was *not* for Jesus to *pay* God, or to *pay* for our sins, but for the Son to assume our humanity, take on the disease, die from it (the consequence of sin is death) and to *beat the disease* - to rise again, victorious, having conquered hell.

And when he rises from the dead, he says, in effect, "I am the antidote to the spiritual disease and its consequences!" "Eat my flesh, drink my blood." We have a *relationship* with God through Christ.

I still have the disease, but I'm getting better, because Christ is in me. And on the last day, I too am going to conquer the disease. I'm going to kick sin and death in the teeth in the resurrection. Not because God was *against* me but has now been appeased by the payment of Christ on the cross, but because God has been *for* me all along. While I was yet a sinner, he loved me. And everyone else, for that matter.

Salvation, then, is not a juridical thing ("Because of Christ I've been moved

from one column to the next, I've been
pronounced innocent though I am guilty"),
not a transactional thing ("I've done the
right things, I've pulled the right lever, I
get the right allotment of forgiveness."),
but a *healing* thing (the Greek word *sozo* is
the word for healing, made whole, *and*
salvation in the New Testament).

Thinking Like The Early Church

If we are saved by the incarnation,
life, death, resurrection, and ascension of
Jesus Christ, what are we saved *from*?
Many modern Christians would quickly
respond, "We are saved from hell." In fact,
this has become a principle focus in most
evangelistic sermons and witnessing.
Interestingly enough, in all the evangelistic
sermons of the Apostles recorded in the
book of Acts, not a single one makes even
the slightest reference to hell. What has
become a mainstay in evangelistic
methodology today was completely foreign
to the Apostles, and as an aside, I would

suggest that either they or we have done it wrong.

Others today might answer, "We are saved from the wrath of God." As if we needed to by saved *by* God *from* God.

I am not discounting the realities of either hell or the wrath of God, but what the early church saw us being saved from was alienation from our Creator. Because of our fallenness, because of sin, because of all kinds of things, humanity as a whole and each of us as individuals were severed from the life giving union with God that we were designed to experience. The end result, according to Scripture, was death, both physical and spiritual.

What *was* preached in all those apostolic sermons in Acts was that "Jesus is Lord" (that is, Jesus is Adonai, Jesus is Jehovah, Jesus is God), and the call was made to enter his kingdom, his lordship, and be transformed by his presence and power through the Holy Spirit at work in our lives. The demonstrable *reason* Jesus was Lord, that is, the way he was *shown* to be Lord, was by his conquering death and hell and his rising from the dead on the third day. A man beat death. A human being got up out of the grave and lives forever, having utterly conquered death. He became, we are told, "the firstfruits" of those who receive his life as their own (1 Corinthians 15.20,23), and we too shall one day defeat death and put on immortality.

Christ conquered sin, death and hell, and now offers himself to us as a kind of spiritual antidote that will transform us to *be like him*. Gregory of Nazianzus believed this was "the unifying thrust of the incarnation...The whole point of the Son's assumption of human existence is to unite it to himself in order to heal and save it."[27]

Salvation then, in a nutshell, is found in being reconciled with God. When St. Paul capsulized the Gospel into single sentence he wrote, "in Christ God was

[27] Beeley, Christopher, *Gregory of Nazianzus on the Trinity and the Knowledge of God*, Oxford, Oxford University Press, 2008, p. 128.

reconciling the world to himself, *not counting their trespasses* against them…" (2 Corinthians 5.19). In the person of Jesus Christ, fully God and fully human, God reconciled the world to himself; reconciled all that he had made; reconciled creation. Something in the cosmos fundamentally changed when God joined himself to his creation in Jesus Christ. Yes, certainly, that is to be worked out and lived out and grown into and declared and proclaimed. But the process of salvation isn't found in keeping rules (however important rules may be). The process of salvation isn't found in doing "the right thing" so God won't be angry with us. This is wrongheaded thinking. The process of salvation is found in *growing in union with God*. The early church called this process *theosis* or *divinization*. We are saved (the Greek word is *sozo* - to be healed, to be rescued, to be made whole) by being *made like God* because we are growing in union with him. Paul writes that the goal of Christ's work for our salvation is that we might "be *conformed* to the *image* of his Son"

(Romans 8.29).[28] God became man to rescue us from death and give us life in him. *This* is our salvation.

Why is it important to understand who Jesus is? Because Jesus shows us the love of God.

Why is it important to understand who Jesus is? Because in Jesus God defeated our mortal enemy.

Why is it important to understand who Jesus is? Because he is our salvation.

Why is it important to understand who Jesus is? Because, "God so loved the world that he that he gave his only Son, that whoever believes in him should not perish but have eternal life" (John 3.16).

---

[28] Interestingly, Paul uses two words in describing the salvific goal God has for believers which we have been studying in relation to Christ himself: *morphe* and *eikon*. We are to be *conformed* (*summorphos*) to the *image* (*eikon*) of his Son.

Chapter Ten

Loose Ends

"But, what about...?"

There are usually four Scriptures that come to people's minds which cause them to struggle with the idea that God the Son is the singular manifestation of God the Father through the procession, presence, and power of God the Holy Spirit.

Jesus' Baptism

> And when Jesus was baptized, immediately he went up from the water, and behold, the heavens were opened to him, and he saw the Spirit of God descending like a dove and coming to rest on him; and behold, a voice from heaven said, "This is my beloved Son, with whom I am well pleased" (Matthew 3.16,17).

At first glance, this story seems to throw a monkey wrench into everything we have said about the Trinity. The witnesses at the river seem to see the Father, the Son, and the Holy Spirit. Indeed, the presence of the Father, Son and the Holy Spirit is evident here. The first thing to say in response is, the Trinity cannot be divided. We *never* encounter the Son without the presence of the Father and the Holy Spirit. But if we pause and think for a minute, what we *see* here is God the Son:

- In the person of the man in the water, Jesus, we see God the Son.

- In the voice coming from the Father in heaven we *hear* the Word of the Lord: the Word coming from the Father, that is, the Son!

- Finally, the Holy Spirit descends "like a dove." Something is *seen* here, something is tangible. Any tangible manifestation of the invisible God is the Son.

Yes, the Trinity is at work here. But God isn't in three "parts." He can't be divided out so that *here* the Son is at work or *there* the Father is doing something or *over there* the Spirit is active. Any time we encounter God we are encountering the fullness of the Trinity, the Father revealing himself through the Son by the energy and presence and procession of the Holy Spirit.

"Father, Son and Holy Spirit are three complete Persons, each of whom not only possesses the fullness of being but is also wholly God. One Hypostasis is not a third of a common essence; it accommodates within itself the entire plenitude of the Divinity. The Father is God, not a third of God. The Son also is God, and so is the Holy Spirit. We confess 'Father, Son and Holy Spirit, Trinity one in essence and undivided.'"[29]

So, when we see the man in the water we see the whole Trinity, when hear the voice from heaven we hear the whole Trinity, when we see the dove descending we see the whole Trinity. The story of Jesus' baptism *is* trinitarian. But it is *not* tritheistic.

Jesus In The Garden

And going a little farther he fell on his face and prayed, saying, "My Father, if it be possible, let this cup pass from me; nevertheless, not as I

---

[29] Alfeyev, Hilarion, *The Mystery of Faith*, London, Darton, Longman & Todd, 2002, p. 35.

will, but as you will" (Matthew 26.39).

It would seem, in the story of Jesus' agony, that we have a juxtaposition of the Son and the Father, the Son willing one thing while the Father wills another. But we must remember that Jesus is fully God *and fully man*. No one likes being tortured. No one enjoys the Spanish Inquisition! The early church made it clear that in the one person of Jesus Christ there were two natures (divine and human), and two wills.

The Third Council of Constantinople in 681 (the sixth of the seven ecumenical councils) declared,

> And we likewise preach two natural wills in him [Jesus Christ], and two natural operations undivided, inconvertible, inseparable, unmixed, according to the doctrine of the holy fathers; and the two natural wills [are] not contrary (as the impious heretics assert), far from it! but his human will follows the divine will,

and is not resisting or reluctant, but rather subject to his divine and omnipotent will. For it was proper that the will of the flesh should be moved, but be subjected to the divine will, according to the wise Athanasius. For as his flesh is called and is the flesh of the God Logos, so is also the natural will of his flesh the proper will of the Logos, as he says himself: 'I came from heaven not to do my own will but the will of the Father who sent me' (John 6:38)... Therefore we confess two natural wills and operations, harmoniously united for the salvation of the human race."

In the Garden of Gethsemane, as a man, Jesus is being "obedient to the point of death" (Philippians 2.8). This is not a case of God the Son having a will different than God the Father. This is a case of a man being filled with angst as the agony of torture and death approached.

Jesus On The Cross

> And about the ninth hour Jesus
> cried out with a loud voice, saying,
> *"Eli, Eli, lema sabachthani?"* that is,
> "My God, my God, why have you
> forsaken me?" (Matthew 27.46).

If Jesus is God, how could God
forsake himself? Some heretics have taught
that Jesus wasn't actually God but was just
a man who "contained" God, and when he
died on the cross God departed from him,
so that he died as a man bereft of the
presence of God. Obviously this idea flies
in the face of the witness of Scripture, but
why did Jesus cry out with these words as
he hung dying?

First, we should note that Jesus, the
whole time he is on the cross, is quoting the
Psalms. Matthew records a line here and a
line there, but this is a man quoting the
Word of God as he suffers agony. The
Gospel writers (and Jesus himself) have a
way of using a kind of shorthand, saying a
single line from Scripture which will

instantly bring to mind an entire passage, an entire story, and entire history, for the original readers. For example, when Jesus says, "So when you see the abomination of desolation spoken of by the prophet Daniel..." (Matthew 24.15), the original readers instantly referenced Daniel chapter nine, the whole story of the prophet Daniel, and the whole story of Antiochus Epiphanes and his desecration of the Temple.[30]

On the cross, Jesus is praying Psalm 22, which begins, "My God, my God, why have you forsaken me?" But this is the *beginning* of the prayer, not the end. The Psalm continues with a tale of agony, "many bulls encompass me...I am poured out like water, and all my bones are out of joint...a company of evildoers encircles me; they have pierced my hands and feet...." But the Psalm, the prayer, *ends* in victory:

---

[30] For a detailed study of Matthew 24, see my *The End Is Near...Or Maybe Not!*, Denison, TX, Mayeux Press, 2011.

But you, O Lord, do not be far off! O you my help, come quickly to my aid...The afflicted shall eat and be satisfied; those who seek him shall praise the Lord...All the ends of the earth shall remember and turn to the Lord...Posterity shall serve him; it shall be told of the Lord to the coming generation; they shall come and proclaim his righteousness to a people yet unborn, that he has done it.

The prayer that begins in despair ends in the hope of victory. Jesus is praying the prayer of his ancestor David, a Psalm about the Messiah, about himself, and he knows the end of the story.

Having said that, in this moment of agony Jesus is also identifying with all who suffer, identifying with the human condition. "Jesus' cry of abandonment, in other words, does not reflect the absence of God in his suffering, but God's inclusion of our abandonment within his saving

embrace and his healing *presence* in the
midst of our desolation and death."[31]

God didn't leave Jesus on the cross.
Jesus was God on the cross.

Stephen's Death

> But he, full of the Holy Spirit, gazed
> into heaven and saw the glory of
> God, and Jesus standing at the right
> hand of God (Acts 7.55).

When the first Christian martyr died
for his faith, with Saul who would become
Paul standing there consenting to his
death, he had a vision of heaven where he

---

[31] Beeley, p. 138. He continues, "Thus for Gregory the
awesome nature of the Christian faith is chiefly 'to see
God crucified' (43.64). It is with this shocking
proclamation that he chooses to end his final oration:
'We needed an incarnate God, a God put to death, so
that we might live, and we were put to death with him';
and so, 'God was crucified' (45.28-29). Because it was
God who died on the cross - the Son of God made
human just for this purpose - his death can be the death
of all fallen humanity, and we can be purified and made
a new creation by his divine life."

saw "Jesus standing at the right hand of God." How could this be, if Jesus is God the Son and is the manifestation of the invisible God?

First, this is a vision, and visions are not to be taken literally (consider all the other visions in the Bible - a sheet full of animals, dragons, seven headed beasts, a floating flaming pot, a multi-metal statue; you get the picture). Visions are usually symbolic, not literal. But beyond this, Luke is using particular Old Testament language that is pregnant with implications.

The right hand is the hand of blessing, the hand of authority, and the hand of power. When Israel blesses his grandsons Ephraim and Manasseh, he crosses his arms and lays his right hand on the younger one, giving him the greater blessing (Genesis 48.14). Moses sang, "Your *right hand*, O Lord, glorious in power, your right hand, O Lord, shatters the enemy" (Exodus 15.6). In his final blessing to the people, Moses recounted how God came to them "from the ten thousands of holy ones, with flaming fire at his *right hand*" (Deuteronomy 33.2). David wrote, "At your *right hand* are pleasures forevermore," and, "Your *right hand* is filled with righteousness," and, *"Give salvation by your right hand* and answer us" (Psalm 16.11, 48.10, 60.5).

Jesus, "standing at the right hand of God" is a reference to Psalm 110.1 (which, along with Psalm 2, is the Psalm most quoted in the New Testament): "The Lord says to my Lord: *'Sit at my right hand*, until I make your enemies your footstool'" Did you notice the double reference to the Lord here? *"The* Lord said to *my* Lord..."

Jesus quotes this verse when he makes the astonishing argument that he is the Messiah, and that he supersedes even great David:

> And as Jesus taught in the temple, he said, "How can the scribes say that the Christ is the son of David? David himself, in the Holy Spirit, declared, 'The Lord said to my Lord,

"Sit at my right hand, until I put your enemies under your feet."'
David himself calls him Lord. So how is he his son?" And the great throng heard him gladly (Mark 12.35-37).

The New Testament writers saw this as the messianic psalm *par excellence*, and used it repeatedly to proclaim that Jesus as the Lord who was given the place of all blessing, authority, power and salvation. When Luke describes Stephen's vision, the text isn't making a theological argument for two different beings who are both God. It is saying that this Jesus, whom Stephen served and was dying for, was actually the Messiah, the Lord of heaven, the long prophesied one, who though crucified but weeks before was now exalted by God,

> ...according to the working of his great might that he worked in Christ when he raised him from the dead and *seated him at his right hand* in the heavenly places far above all rule and authority and power and

dominion, and above every name
that is named, not only in this age
but also in the one to come
(Ephesians 1.19-21; cf. Ephesians
2.6, Colossians 3.1, Hebrews 8.1,
12.2,).

Jesus, the fully human one, is God's
"right hand man."

A Final Word

If the study of God remains nothing
more than a cerebral exercise it has not
accomplished its purpose. The goal is to
know God, and to be known by him. The
goal that the Holy Trinity has for humanity
is that we might know him, be in union
with him, and be made whole by him. This
is why God became man - for us and for
our salvation.

"Every human being is recreated and
renewed in Christ. The redemptive
act of Christ was not accomplished
for an abstract 'mass' of people, but

for every single individual. As St. Symeon says, 'God sent his only-begotten Son to earth for you and for your salvation, for he has seen you and destined you to be his brother and co-heir…'

"…It is in Christ that the purpose of human existence is realized: communion with God, union with God, deification…In his immeasurable love for us Christ ascended Golgotha and endured death on the Cross, which reconciled and united the human race with God."[32]

And that, my friends, is good news.

---

[32] Alfeyev, p. 91f.

Bibliography

Alfeyev, Hilarion, *The Mystery of Faith*, London, Darton, Longman & Todd, 2002.

Barth, Karl, *Church Dogmatics*, Volume 1; Edinburg, T & T Clark, 1960.

Barth, Karl, *The Göttingen Dogmatics: Instruction in the Christian Religion*, Grand Rapids, Eerdmans, 1991.

Beeley, Christopher A., *Gregory of Nazianzus on the Trinity and the Knowledge of God*, Oxford, Oxford University Press, 2008.

Bruner, Emil, *The Christian Doctrine of God*, Philadelphia, Westminster Press, 1946.

Chesterton, Gilbert Keith, *The Collected Works of G.K. Chesterton, Volume 1*, San Francisco, Ignatius Press, 1986.

Fortmann, Edmund J., *The Triune God*, Grand Rapids, Baker, 1972.

Jungel, Eberhard, *The Doctrine Of The Trinity*, Grand Rapids, Eardmans, 1976.

Kittel, Gerhard, *Theological Dictionary of the New Testament*, 10 Volumes, Grand Rapids, Eerdmans, 1977.

Oden, Thomas C., *The Living God*, Peabody, MA, Hendrickson Publishers, 1987.

Oden, Thomas C., editor, *Ancient Christian Doctrine, Volume One: We Believe In One God*, Downers Grove, IL, InterVarsity Press, 2009.

Oden, Thomas C., editor, *Ancient Christian Doctrine, Volume Two: We Believe in One Lord Jesus Christ*, Downers Grove, IL, InterVarsity Press, 2009.

Olson, Roger E., *The Story of Christian Theology*, Downers Grove, IL, InterVarsity Press, 1999. Rusch, William G., *The Trinitarian Controversy*, Philadelphia, Fortress Press, 1980.

Schaff, Philip, *The Ante-Nicene Fathers, 10 Volumes*, Peabody, MA, Hendrickson Publishers, 1994.

Schaff, Philip, *The Nicene and Post-Nicene Fathers, 14 Volumes*, Peabody, MA, Hendrickson Publishers, 1996.

Spurgeon, Charles, *The Treasury of David*, Houston, Pilgrim Publications, 1983.

Thayer, Joseph Henry, *Greek-English Lexicon of the New Testament*, Grand Rapids, Zondervan, 1974.

Tillich, Paul, *A History of Christian Thought*, New York, Simon and Schuster, 1967.

About the Author

Kenneth Myers was born in 1959 in Denison, Texas. The son of a pastor/missionary, he married Shirley McSorley in 1977. They have three children and five grandchildren. He is an Anglican bishop and director of Graceworks Teaching Ministry.

www.kennethmyers.net

Made in the USA
Columbia, SC
11 July 2024